Twayne's English Authors Series

EDITOR OF THIS VOLUME

Bertram Davis

Florida State University

William Law

TEAS 282

THE

WORKS

Of the REVEREND

WILLIAM LAW, A. M.

In NINE VOLUMES.

VOL. I.

CONTAINING

Three LETTERS to the Bishop
of *Bangor*.

LONDON:

Printed for J. RICHARDSON, in *Pater-Noster-Row.*
MDCCLXII.

Photo of the title page of the first edition of William Law's works, privately printed in 1762.

WILLIAM LAW

By ERWIN PAUL RUDOLPH

Wheaton College

TWAYNE PUBLISHERS

A DIVISION OF G. K. HALL & CO., BOSTON

Copyright © 1980 by G. K. Hall & Co.

Published in 1980 by Twayne Publishers,
A Division of G. K. Hall & Co.
All Rights Reserved

Printed on permanent/durable acid-free paper and bound
in the United States of America

First Printing

Library of Congress Cataloging in Publication Data

Rudolph, Erwin Paul.
William Law.

(Twayne's English authors series; TEAS 282)
Bibliography: p. 149–51
Includes index.
1. Law, William, 1686–1761.
BV5095.L3R36   1980   230'.3   80–16350
ISBN 0-8057-6765-7

Contents

About the Author

Preface

Chronology

1. The Man and His Times   13

2. The Early Works of Devotion: *Christian Perfection* and *A Serious Call*   24

3. Nondevotional Works: Controversy and Theology   55

4. The "Later" Law   82

5. Law's Enduring Achievement   109

Notes and References   135

Selected Bibliography   149

Index   152

About the Author

Erwin Paul Rudolph received his B.A. from Greenville College, and his M.A. in English literature from Ohio State University. From 1941 to 1953 he was an ordained minister in the Free Methodist Church of North America. Professor Rudolph received his Ph.D. in English literature from the University of Illinois in 1962. His special fields are Medieval and Eighteenth Century English literature. Professor Rudolph is currently teaching at Wheaton College in Illinois. His publications include articles on Dante Alighieri and John Ruskin in *The New International Dictionary of the Christian Church*. He edited an edition of *Christian Perfection* by William Law, and has also edited several books in the Great Christian Classics Series (Wheaton, Victor Books).

Preface

The present study calls attention to William Law as preeminently a writer of Christian devotion. Other studies have treated him as theologian, controversialist and Non-juror, or mystic. Occasionally, *Christian Perfection* and *A Serious Call to a Devout and Holy Life* may be referred to as general treatises on devotion; however, Law's unique kinship with earlier outstanding contributors to the tradition of devotional prose literature has not been sufficiently underscored or demonstrated. Yet anyone who reads Law seriously will not fail to see that he belongs with such writers as St. Augustine, Francis de Sales, the author of *The Cloud of Unknowing*, Jeremy Taylor, and Lancelot Andrewes, who have distinguished themselves in that literary genre.

That a sizable body of this literature existed before Law has been generally recognized.[1] Unfortunately, however, the term "devotional literature" has not always been well defined, but has been used broadly to refer to religious literature of a more general sort. It will be useful, therefore, to point out early the distinguishing characteristics of that species of literature to determine what Law has in common with his devotional predecessors and the extent to which he is affected by them.

The principal aim here is to show that the traditional, identifying features of devotional prose are prominent in Law's works; to note that the devotional strain remains uppermost in his writings even after he encounters mystical influences; and to show that his able treatment of devotional themes, together with his achievement as prose stylist and his influence upon others, earns for him a prominent place in the tradition of devotional prose. While the entire range of Law's thought will be examined, the works that are not of one piece with the devotional writing will not be stressed, as they do not constitute his major achievement.

A brief sketch of Law's life in relation to his times is intended as a helpful introduction to this comparatively little-known writer. Even the outlines of his life illustrate the piety he recommends in his works. The second chapter links the "early" works, *Christian Perfection* and *A Serious Call*, with the devotional tradition by a discussion of the themes they have in common. A definition of "devotional literature" introduces this section.

Chapter three describes and analyzes the nondevotional writings. These works are primarily controversial and theological and are directed to the religious and philosophical issues of Law's own time. Even here, however, one discerns the same incisively pious mind at work; the same intensely moral outlook is everywhere evident.

The "later" Law, illustrated by *The Spirit of Love*, *The Spirit of Prayer*, and *The Way to Divine Knowledge*, provides studies in devotion after Law's major encounter with Jacob Boehme and other mystics. The association of mysticism with these works has frequently provoked criticism of Law for his alleged defection from orthodoxy. But those who criticize Law for his mysticism usually fail to dissociate him from the extremists of that school or to note how mysticism pervades the thought of most devotional writers. The alteration in Law's thought is more a change in emphasis than in basic belief, for he never renounces his former doctrinal position, and the same devotional themes and pious tone are everywhere evident. If one considers intuitive approach to reality, the awareness of unity in diversity, the passion for the spirituality that underlies and unifies all things to be the essentials of mysticism, one recognizes readily that these are the principal concerns of the devotional writer as well. Law's "change" is therefore more apparent than real.

Underneath the vitality and unremitting earnestness of the writers of devotional prose is a sensitivity to style. Chapter five points up Law's simplicity, pungency, and vividness of expression and some of the influence he has exerted on such leading figures as Samuel Johnson and John Wesley.

Although the tradition of devotional literature goes back to early beginnings, the themes and worshipful manner continue unabated from century to century and transcend time and place. Any serious review of literature that is concerned primarily with God's intimate dealings with the human soul must take into account the devotional writings of William Law, for he spoke as clearly concerning the ways and means of worship as anyone before him or since.

Paradoxically, the perennial influence claimed for Law is over-matched by his obscurity. The research done on him has been comparatively meager. However, a few significant studies in the past thirty-five years suggest a renewed interest in him. Time has a way of reassessing a writer's achievement. It may be that after two hundred years we are better able to judge Law's impact upon the world as writer and thinker. Possibly, too, his steady voice of religious faith provides reassurance for an apprehensive age that sees elsewhere little basis for optimism in the face of present world disorders. It is hoped that the general reader, as well as the specialist, will find in him new wisdom and insight.

Chronology

1686   William Law born at King's Cliffe, Northampton, fourth of eight sons in a family of eleven children.

1705   Entered Emmanuel College, Cambridge, as a Sizar.

1708   Received his B.A. degree.

1711   Became Fellow of Emmanuel College and was ordained deacon.

1712   Received the M.A. degree.

1713   Preached *Sermon on the Peace of 1713* at Haslingfield, where Law probably was curate from 1711 to 1713.

1714   Refused to take oath of allegiance to George I; death of his father.

1716   Law as a Non-juror lost his Fellowship and left Cambridge.

1717–   Wrote *Three Letters to the Bishop of Bangor.*
1719

1718   Death of his mother.

1723   Employed as tutor in the household of Edward Gibbon, father of the historian; lived at Putney and Cambridge. Wrote *Remarks Upon the Fable of the Bees*, a refutation of Bernard Mandeville's work.

1726   Wrote *The Unlawfulness of Stage Entertainment* and *A Treatise Upon Christian Perfection.*

1727   Ordained priest by Non-juror Bishop Gandy; founded a girl's school at King's Cliffe.

1729   Wrote *A Serious Call to a Devout and Holy Life.* John Byrom's first visit to Law (Putney).

1731   Wrote *The Case of Reason or Natural Religion.*

1731–   Wrote *Letters to a Lady Inclined to Enter . . . the Church*
1732   *of Rome.*

1732   Law's first visit from John Wesley.

1734   Edward Gibbon left Cambridge; Law remained at Putney.

ca. 1735   Began to read Jacob Boehme.

1736   Wrote *Letters to Fanny Henshaw*; controversy with the Quakers.

1737   Wrote *A Demonstration of the Gross and Fundamental Errors of a Late Book Called 'A Plain Account of the Nature and End of the Sacrament of the Lord's Supper.'* Law's relation with the Gibbons was dissolved with the death of Edward Gibbon, Sr.

1738   Breach with John Wesley; Wesley's Aldersgate experience.

1738–   Residence in London.
1739

1739   Began residence at King's Cliffe. Wrote *The Grounds and Reasons for Christian Regeneration.*

1740   Wrote *An Appeal to All Who Doubt the Truths of the Gospel* and *An Answer to Dr. Trapp's Discourse* (and *Some Animadversions on Dr. Trapp's Reply*).

1743   Visited by Byrom at King's Cliffe.

1749–   Wrote *The Spirit of Prayer.*
1750

1752   Wrote *The Way to Divine Knowledge.* King's Cliffe Library founded.

1752–   Wrote *The Spirit of Love.*
1754

1756   Wesley's open *Letter to the Rev. William Law* criticizing the latter's 1752–54 works. Law built a school and almshouses.

1757   Wrote *A Confutation of Dr. Warburton's Projected Defence of Christianity.*

1760   Wrote *A Dialogue on Justification* and *A Collection of Letters.* . . .

1761   Wrote *An Address to the Clergy.* On April 9 William Law died.

CHAPTER 1

The Man and His Times

BORN at King's Cliffe, near Stanford, Northamptonshire, in 1686, the fourth of eight sons in a family of eleven children, William Law came from a background "of high respectability and of good means."[1] The quiet, unpretentious village into which he was born hardly reflected the fantastic energy of the eighteenth century any more than it did the seething violence of the seventeenth. Few details are known of his early years, but his entering Emmanuel College, Cambridge, as Sizar in 1705 gave evidence of his early plans to enter the ministry of the Church of England.[2] He must have shown considerable promise as a young student, for as far as we know he was the only one of the children whom his father sent to the university. He received the B.A. degree in 1708, a Fellowship to Emmanuel College in 1711 (the same year in which he was ordained), and the M.A. in 1712. A conscientious reader while at the university, according to Byrom, Law's personal friend and journalist, he gave diligent attention to the reading of the classics, philosophy, Hebrew, and French. He probably became familiar with numerous writings of the Church Fathers, a few of the fourteenth-century English mystics, and such devotional writers as St. Francis de Sales, François Fenelon, and Thomas à Kempis.[3] In addition, he was a student of science and the philosophy of Descartes, an admirer of St. Augustine and Plato, and at the same time a loyal son of the Church. At Cambridge he became interested in the thought of Nicholas Malebranche and wrote a thesis on that French Cartesian philosopher.

There is no evidence that Law participated actively in the political controversies of the day. But his "tripos" speech, made at a public meeting at the University in 1713, in which he allegedly reflected on the government; his 1713 sermon in defense of the Treaty of Utrecht, the Queen, and the Divine Right; and his refusal to take the oaths of allegiance and abjuration upon the accession of George I in 1714—

these exemplified his determination to put personal conviction above convenience, even though that course meant the loss of his Fellowship at Cambridge and permanent denial of the right to serve as a minister in the Church of England.

Law had gone to Cambridge in the third year of Queen Anne's reign. After the death of Anne in 1714 he made a decision that was to affect his whole life. His sensitive conscience prompted him to join the ranks of those who refused the Hanoverian claim to the English throne. The Non-jurors were not militant rebels; they were conscientious objectors who preferred to deny themselves official positions for obscure places of service.[4]

Law had no political ambition. The secluded life to which he withdrew gave him opportunity to write his works of spiritual admonition. His decision not to go on with the career for which he had prepared himself caused him some distress, as he indicates in a letter to his brother:

My prospect indeed is melancholy enough, but had I done what was required of me to avoid it, I should have thought my condition much worse. The benefits of my education seem partly at an end, but that same education had been miserably lost if I had not learnt to fear something more than misfortune.[5]

Law did not swerve, however, from his determined course of action, nor did deprivation of a formal church assignment create in him bitterness or rancor, for he continued to attend regularly his parish church and refrained from recriminatory remarks against churchmen who opposed his position as Non-juror.

A gap appears in Law's biography after he left the University, but we know that his father died in 1714 and his mother in 1718, and that by 1723 he was back at Cambridge with young Edward Gibbon, the father of the historian.[6] Thereafter he served regularly in the Gibbon household at Putney as private tutor and chaplain. Upon the death of the elder Gibbon in 1739 this relationship was dissolved.

Law's stay in London (1738–39) was too brief to afford him much contact with the intellectuals who were frequenting the coffeehouses and literary clubs of the "Town." But we have little assurance that he would have made much effort to meet with such men even if he had had ample opportunity, for as he stated in the rules he outlined for himself at the University, he felt disinclined to seek out "public houses." He did meet periodically with a coterie of disciples, including John Wesley and John Byrom, and we may assume that he had occasion to greet distinguished guests in the Gibbon home. But his main preoccupation was other-worldly. In fact, to read any part of his biography is to encounter the devotional strain that impregnates his entire life and thought. As theologian Robert Flew puts it, "His life of purity and self-denial is of one piece with his devotional writings."[7] Few men have exemplified more completely than he how to desire nothing in this world but to do the will of God. His primary interests, therefore, lay outside the mainstream of public life.

At the close of his London period, Law took up permanent residence in King's Cliffe, a modest but charming rural setting, where his introspective habits and practical charity continued to exemplify the high standards of piety recommended in his writings. A school for orphan girls, which he had founded in 1727, he now supervised personally; he also distributed food and clothing daily to the poor of the community, illustrating further his determination to practice the benevolence he enjoined. In addition, he served as spiritual adviser to two well-bred women, Miss Hester Gibbon, aunt of the historian, and Mrs. Sarah Hutcheson, whose husband recommended that upon his decease she place herself under the spiritual direction of Mr. Law. Later the trio founded two almshouses and a school for boys.[8]

A lengthy account by Christopher Walton of the daily rounds of activity at King's Cliffe indicates the pious rule and discipline that guided Law's life and that corresponded to the severity of his teachings.[9] Law arose each morning about five o'clock, spent some time in devotion "after which he breakfasted, generally on a cup of chocolate in his bedroom, and then commenced study." At nine o'clock a bell was rung for family devotions after which Law passed the remainder of the forenoon with his books. He dined at noon in winter and at one in summer, partaking very moderately and "allowing himself one glass of wine." After dinner he and his companions Hester Gibbon and Sarah Hutcheson usually assembled for devotional exercises, following which Law again retired to his study until tea-time. After tea, exercises of piety were resumed, "often with the servants in turn reading a chapter from the Bible." Law also gave attention to the poor of his community. He distributed milk every morning "with his own hands" from the four cows he kept and gave "either of money, apparel, or food" wherever there was need. He insisted that all the clothing given out be clean and in good repair and that the food be appetizing. At times he would interrupt his studies to taste the broth which had been prepared. There were occasional complaints that unworthy mendicants took advantage of his philanthropy.[10]

About twice a week Law went horseback riding with Mrs.

Hutcheson, Miss Gibbon, and some neighbors. Their diversions, however, were few and their outer lives consisted mainly of acts of charity, personal devotion, and storing their minds with the writings of ancient divines. They were also regular in their church attendance.

Law's attention to his devotional life at King's Cliffe is exemplified further by his collecting a manuscript of choice forms of devotion, including confessions, petitions, and praises from the psalter and arranging them topically for his own use. Such constancy in devotion may have resulted partially, as Alexander Whyte suggests, from Law's earlier controversial activity; after his early encounters with the unorthodox writings of Benjamin Hoadley, Bernard Mandeville, and Matthew Tindal, he probably felt the need for a renewal of personal humility. But clearly, while he admonished others continually in his works to improve their spiritual lives, like Chaucer's Parson, he first practiced a pious rule himself.

Law lived out his days at King's Cliffe seeking to please God in his daily rounds of ordinary duties. Unto the very end of his life he manifested a devout spirit to those about him:

Mr. Law lived to the age of seventy-five without the infirmities of age. . . . His eye was still piercing, for it was the organ of his immortal soul filled with Divine light. His heart was filled with God, and therefore his voice was the sweet trumpeter of Divine love.[11]

After catching a cold at the annual audit of the school accounts during Easter week in 1761, he developed a kidney inflammation, which resulted in his death in less than a fortnight. According to Miss Gibbon, every word he spoke during his affliction was of joy and divine transport, and he died singing a hymn.

No authentic portrait of Law exists, but Walton's description of his physical appearance and personal habits provides additional insight into the manner and purpose that characterized his whole life:

In stature, Mr. Law was rather over than under middle size; his frame was not corpulent, but stoutly built, and kept in healthy action by the unflinching discipline and regularity of habits. The general form of his countenance was round; and he possessed a blunt felicitous readiness of utterance. He had well-proportioned features, which were recommended by a cheerful, open expression, and probably became more decided as he advanced in years, the natural effect of his strong judgment and of the studious gravity of his youth. His face was ruddy; his eyes grey, clear, vivacious, sparkling with noble benignity, and with the keen wit which his writings testify, was always ruled like a well-broken but generous stud, by his superior wisdom.

His general manner was lively and unaffected, and though his walk and conversation among his friends was that of a sage, we have the testimony . . . that he was accustomed to see company, and was a man of free conversation. . . . Perhaps the gravity of his looks and demeanor was a little heightened by the soberness of his dress, which was usually a clerical hat, with the loops let down, black coat, and grey wig.[12]

The intensely devout life of William Law may have made a lasting impression upon many who knew him, but the nine volumes of his writings stand as the true monument to his lasting achievement. Although interest here centers primarily upon Law's devotional works, one cannot fail to see in all that he wrote the same "unity of righteousness," the same religious mind at work, fondling themes that were dear to him and turning again and again upon the spiritual discipline that characterized his determination to know the truth about himself and his responsibility to a Superior Being.

In some ways William Law was a child of his times, but in more notable ways he stood alone and quite apart from them. Generally, the eighteenth century was marked by an increase in religious toleration. Divisions in religion, the chief causes of wars since the Reformation, began to be endured more patiently by statesmen who now realized that differences could not be abolished. Although the Parliament of 1661 was at first intolerant because it remembered the harshness of the Puritans and feared what would happen to the constitution if its opponents should get into power, it allowed concessions gradually to the many competing religious bodies as they began to recognize that they had to learn to coexist. Most of the populace still dreaded a return to Puritan rule, however, while others feared the establishment of Roman Catholicism.

At the end of the seventeenth century churchmen devoted to the House of Stuart's hereditary rights were reluctant to transfer allegiance to King William, particularly when he sought to impose a new Prayer Book on the Church by authority of the state. However, the Toleration Act of 1689 relieved some of the religious tension. All Protestant Trinitarian Nonconformists were allowed to worship as they chose, provided their meetings remained open to the public and their ministers subscribed to the Thirty-Nine Articles (which did not deal with the doctrine or organization of the Church). Although the Non-jurors later alienated themselves at the accession of the Hanoverians, most of the church bodies recognized that the differences between Anglican, Catholic, and Independent were fundamental enough to command mutual respect.

The prevalence of controversy, another feature of the early eighteenth century, may appear inconsistent with the disposition toward toleration. Yet toleration did not mean that strong differences of opinion did not exist. Although less bitterly partisan than in the preceding century, many of the Anglicans, Catholics, and Independents alike were still quick to challenge openly any departure from their cherished beliefs. The century witnessed the Bangorian controversy, ending with the silencing of the Convocation; the Nonjuror controversy; the Jacobite controversy, ending with the trial and banishment of Bishop Atterbury; and the Trinitarian, Arian, and Deistic controversies. These engaged the leading religious minds of the day: Benjamin Hoadley, a notable bishop of the Established Church, excited the antagonism of his contemporaries by his indifference to the historical claims of the church and his lack of sympathy with the Thirty-Nine Articles or Book of Common Prayer. His insistence on the supremacy of reason in faith and practice, his denunciation of enthusiasm, and his urging of enlightened refinement and the decorous life were all combined to discount church authority. William Law himself was drawn into a reply to Hoadley's arguments; and the Deists, with their emphasis upon the validity of natural religion, drew into public argument not only philosophers like Thomas Hobbes and the Earl of Shaftesbury and statesmen like Bolingbroke, but also such churchmen as Samuel Clarke, Joseph Butler, and, later in the century, William Paley.

Sometimes the century's religious life is portrayed as lethargic and worldly:

It is a period . . . of lethargy instead of activity, of worldiness instead of self-denial, of grossness instead of refinement. There was groveling instead of a noble conception of the nature and function of the Church as a Christian society, an ignoring of a conscientious and worthy carrying out of the plain system of the Church, work neglected instead of work well done.[13]

Gambling and drinking were prevalent, and masses of the poor, particularly in the rural and slum areas, remained in ignorance. Naturally William Law's puritan demeanor was set in rigid opposition to every grossly sinful practice he detected in English life.

It is also true that exaggerations frequently mark the descriptions of the worldliness of the times. While certain sections of society continued to follow the loose manner set by a Restoration Court dominated by French influence, many God-fearing men withstood faithfully the encroachment of worldliness upon the church. William K. Clarke states that the records for the Society for the Promotion of Christian Knowledge (SPCK) do not bear out the contention that the church was altogether complacent in the eighteenth century: "We get the impression of a militant church, fighting for its life against unbelief and coarse and dissolute manners, depressed at times by the magnitude of its task, but fully conscious both of the evil it was facing and of its impotence to face it in its own strength."[14] Historian George Trevelyan agrees with this view:

It is a common error to regard the eighteenth century in England as irreligious. An ethical code based on Christian doctrine was a rule of life to a much larger proportion of the community than it had been in the late Medieval or Tudor periods. Indeed, the age of Wesley, Cowper, and Dr. Johnson was perhaps as "religious" as the seventeenth century itself, though it had ceased to fight with the sword about rival doctrines of Christianity, and was, therefore, somewhat tolerant of still wider differences of opinion.[15]

This age also saw numerous faithful children of the church, such as Sir Christopher Wren, Lord Dartmouth, and Robert Nelson. That the reading of works of piety had not ceased was indicated by the continual reading in some quarters of such works of devotion from the preceding century as Cosin's *Devotions* or *The Whole Duty of Man* and Jeremy Taylor's *Holy Living* and *Holy Dying*.[16] Other evidence for the vigorous life of the church may be seen in the formation of special groups for the promotion of spiritual life: the Society for the Propagation of the Gospel, begun in 1701, and the Society for Promoting Christian Knowledge, formed in 1698.

The early eighteenth-century satirical turn of mind, which first was leveled at dullness and hypocrisy, attacked all kinds of eccentricity, including strong emotion and unrestrained zeal. Writers were particularly given to social laughter and ridicule. As Addison states, his age surpassed the ancients in "Doggerel, Humour, Burlesque, and all the trivial arts of Ridicule." The period distrusted "enthusiasm" and mysticism in religion and can hardly be called religious in the traditional sense. The recoil from seventeenth-century religious excesses at times imparted a tone of impiety to the fashionable life and literature of the first decades, where greater attention was given to human things than to divine.

Although some writers may be almost entirely the products of their age, it is equally true that others may be the molders of society as well.

William Law was sympathetic with some of the ideas in vogue in his
century, but in many respects he was opposed to the prevailing
religious and intellectual tendencies around him. Through his
controversial writings he attacked those who he felt were opposing
well-established beliefs; through these he also manifested a high
regard for man's rational faculty. His general distaste for what he
believed to be aberrations from religious norms displays a harmony
with the Augustan temper. On the other hand, he belonged to that
company who resisted stubbornly the liberalizing of the evangelical
position and who achieved notable success among both Anglicans
and Nonconformists in arousing passive consciences and stimulating
personal devotion. Even when Law emphasized the place of reason in
religion, he was less extreme than many defenders of biblical
revelation who sought to establish that Christianity was "a replica-
tion of natural religion, with additional authority and penal sanctions."[17]

The intellectual temper that thrived on controversy and inclined to
believe only the evidence of the senses can hardly be expected to
provide a favorable climate for works of pious meditation and
worship. And if, as some aver, this age of controversy was consonant
with a lowering of the tone of the clergy and a general decline of piety
among the laity, one can expect logically a decline in the production
of significant writings of devotion in that period. While there exists as
yet no exhaustive survey of devotional works produced in the early
eighteenth century, the records of the SPCK, which contain a
catalogue of the books dispersed by that society among the adherents
of the Church of England, list dozens of published books and
monographs touching upon doctrine, practical religion, and devotion. Ronald Knox also notes that in addition to such devotional
works as Taylor's *Holy Living* and *Holy Dying*, Richard Baxter's
Saints' Everlasting Rest, and John Bunyan's *Pilgrim's Progress* and
Grace Abounding, which continued to be popular in Law's day, the
eighteenth century produced a flood of monographs on the interior
life, biographies of souls, and books of popular devotion.[18] Thus
while the general public appetite for these books may not have been
as keen as in the preceding century, the eighteenth century was by no
means devoid of works of pious thought and meditation. And Law's
practical treatises on religion were among the best-known devotional
writings produced in the century.

Law must have been fully aware of the eighteenth-century fondness
for testing the reasonableness of well-known religious assumptions.

To prove that the church teachings were true because they were reasonable was the special work of such Latitudinarians as Gilbert Burnet, Edward Stillingfleet, and Thomas Tenison:

To assert the reasonableness of the Church, to prove that religion is agreeable to common sense, and that the practice of virtue brings its own reward even in this life, to depreciate excitement, to denounce the dangers of fanaticism, to disprove the reality of special spiritual illumination, to insist upon the excellence of moderation—such were the lessons which the eighteenth century Latitudinarians had to teach.[19]

The Deists joined in the insistence that religious truth ought to be subjected to the test of reason. The fact of Revelation was not always denied, but the controversy turned upon evidence for it and whether it added anything to the truths of natural religion.[20] Sometimes theologians like Samuel Clarke rehearsed the evidences for Revelation found in the world about them. John Locke, who based all knowledge upon sensation and reflection, accepted Revelation only because he thought that there was sufficient external evidence to support it. George Berkeley, Joseph Butler, and David Hume were also concerned with the foundations of natural religion.[21]

The triumph of natural religion over revealed religion reduced Revelation to a concomitant of faith, lessened the stress on asceticism and original sin, and equated religious life with the practice of virtue. Quite generally, the century was more impressed by the value of the present than by its debt to the past. Consequently, the rational grounds for individual belief became more and more the main subject of discussion.[22] As Mark Pattison points out in his religious symposium, the appeal to reason was "a first effort of English theology to find a new basis for doctrine to replace the foundations which has failed it."[23]

Law was confident, as were many of his contemporaries, that biblical revelation was consonant with a reasonable way of life and urged his readers continually to accept his precepts because they were logically credible. In fact, Law's insistence in both his controversial and devotional works upon an intellectual examination of the tenets of religion reflects a healthy tendency to provide an intellectual foundation for faith at a time when religious enthusiasm was on the rise. The rationalist preachers, with their stress upon the intellectual basis for religious faith, are usually contrasted with the Evangelical pulpit that displaced them. The debt of the latter to the former, however, is not always recognized. As historians John Overton and

Frederic Relton maintain, "The Evangelical movement could never have been the force it was unless it had been preceded by the work which was done most effectually by those who placed Christianity upon a thoroughly firm intellectual basis."[24]

Some of the religious controversies of the period, although providing no congenial climate for devotional literature, at least caused their contributors to rethink and fortify old dogmas with new arguments. Samuel Clarke and David Waterland, for example, in their duel in the Trinitarian controversy over which person in the Godhead is supreme—through their intellectual examination of the basis of the doctrine of the Trinity—helped to focus upon doctrinal soundness rather than emotionalism as a foundation for religious faith. Similarly, Joseph Butler, whose *Analogy of Religion* provided an argument for theism and for the moral purpose of the world, aimed to satisfy the intellectual curiosity and appealed to the rational element in a society that insisted upon knowing *why* religion was needed. Law himself constantly strove to supply logical argument for the doctrines which he recommended. His *Three Letters to the Bishop of Bangor* and *Remarks on the Fable of the Bees*, for example, illustrate this logical manner, which he continued throughout his writings.[25]

An intellectual age that produced writers like Daniel Defoe, Jonathan Swift, Alexander Pope, and Samuel Johnson was bound to affect Law's thought and outlook. In his conservative views upon church affiliation, his admiration for the well-disciplined life, his affection for reason, and his penchant for religious controversy, Law was a child of the eighteenth century. But it is striking that amid the complexity of the times his thoughts traveled continually to heaven, and he consumed his energies depicting the spiritual reality that impressed him directly.

Widely divergent from the views of the Latitudinarian, Law's views upon religion were austere and dogmatic. His identification with the Non-jurors, who were willing to forego ordination in the Anglican Church rather than to compromise their convictions, portrayed his determination to obey the dictates of a sensitive conscience. His treatises upon religion, as well as his writings of religious controversy, bear the stamp of a man who held rigorous religious opinions. At the same time, his appeal to fervency of faith was equally as strong as his emphasis upon the place of reason in a well-ordered religious life.

A satirical turn of mind and emphasis upon reason, which tend to ignore the importance of the mysteries of the Christian faith, are also inimical to a literature that thrives on faith and warm personal devotion. Compared to the vast outpouring of devotional writing during the preceding period, the eighteenth century produced comparatively few persons who resisted stoutly any decline in spiritual life. William Law was foremost among the notable exceptions.

CHAPTER 2

The Early Works of Devotion:
Christian Perfection *and*
A Serious Call

I   *Devotional Literature: A Definition*

O F the many categories of religious writings that emerged between
the discovery of printing and the beginning of the eighteenth
century, none is more conspicuous than what is commonly called
"devotional." As F. A. Gasquet points out in his survey of printed
religious literature in England to 1510, "What must strike every
observer on examining the literature published by our printers in
England, or by foreign printers for the English market, is the great
number of religious and devotional books."[1] An analysis of English
books from 1480 to 1640 reveals that "in some years religious writings
account for more than half of the works published, of which a
considerable number may be labeled 'devotional.'"[2] Religious and
devotional prose continued to hold a prominent place in the writings
of the seventeenth century, as Helen White points out in her significant study.[3]

From the widespread use of the term "devotional" one would
assume that a fairly clear definition for it must exist. A closer
examination, however, reveals that the term is often used in a general
sense to apply to diverse religious literature.[4]

One writer attempts to classify early seventeenth-century devotional writings as (1) collections of prayers, accompanied by sentence
meditation or reflection, (2) books of meditations, (3) selections from
Scripture, (4) treatises on prayer, (5) general devotional books. The
first four of these recognize such acts of piety as prayer or meditation
as constituting the common acts of devotion. However, the last
admits devotional books of a more general sort "in which the interest

in pure devotion is incidental to a treatment of the whole problem of the spiritual life."[5] Such a broad use of the term makes it essential to look for some identifiable features that give this literature a homogeneous quality.

A general examination of Law's devotional predecessors reveals their primary intention to show the reader ways and means by which he may fashion his life to please God. To gain acceptance with God, to commune with God directly, and finally to gain union with Him are their main concerns.

Not designed primarily to inform or to educate, devotional writing "concerns itself with the inner life of man and considers ways and means to strengthen the reality of the union between God and man as far as it is possible in this life."[6] Generally concerned with universal subjects rather than immediate political, social, or religious events, this literature speaks of intangible values that invariably transcend time and place. Because it describes some of the loftiest concepts and aspirations known to man, it excites the imagination and challenges the idealism of the reader. Because the writer is emotionally involved with his subject, he often displays an "affective strain" quite different from that found in a doctrinal treatise or speculative tract. Assuming a general knowledge of religious doctrine, and intent upon securing the practice of principles of the Christian life, he aims to elicit assent of the will through emotional appeal or rhetorical devices designed to persuade the reader to pursue righteous conduct.

Devotional literature is not concerned with religious controversy; therefore, writings of a polemical nature, even though they deal strictly with religious matters, do not belong to the genre. Speculative or theological writings that teach doctrine *per se*, or that aim merely to inform the reader about Christian dogma more than to aid him in achieving personal piety, hardly qualify as devotional writing. Even those sermons that are highly theological, that are addressed more to the mind than to the heart, should not be considered devotional in the strictest sense. Religious writing in general, therefore, is not devotional unless it aims directly at spiritual betterment.

As used in the present study, the term "devotional literature" refers to that body of literature which has as its controlling purpose the aiding of man in his quest of the "godly life." It is concerned with both the motives of piety and the overt acts of worship. Naturally, different writers may vary their emphases, and the devotional tone will be much more readily discernible in some than in others. Yet the impulse to worship provides the motivating force behind these writings.

A devotional work may, of course, be read and appreciated without the reader's assuming the posture or accepting the practice recommended; however, one can hardly fail to recognize at least the dominant intention of the author to assist the spirit and practice of worship or to admit the conceptions of God that inspire the work. Devotional tone helps one to distinguish it from more general religious writing. Ways and means of achieving perfection, gaining acceptance with God, and discerning clearly the implications of worship are the dominant preoccupations which help to give it a devotional tone. Simply to know a religious creed is not enough. There must be a concern for the inner life of the spirit and emulation of the pattern of life that religion propagates.

At least three general characteristics also contribute toward this reverent and worshipful spirit or tone: unremitting moral earnestness, preoccupation with and solicitation to worship, and acceptance of general theological assumptions that have to do with the nature of God, the depravity of man, and the possibility of grace.

One cannot read far into devotional literature without sensing the contagion of righteousness that pervades it. The logical consequence of the basic philosophies of these writers, who made the main concern of their lives the emulation of the life of God and inquiry into the inner life of man, was to impart an inescapable moral earnestness to their works. Whether or not one agrees with the writers' convictions or is moved to alter his conduct, he cannot help seeing that here at least were some who were intent upon ordering the practical concerns of everyday life in accord with eternal interests. To read the works of St. Augustine or Richard Baxter or Thomas Becon or William Law is to sense the unpretentious spirit of men who made piety and worship the main business of their lives.

Another source of devotional tone in the writings here reviewed may be found in the theological assumptions that underlie them. Admittedly, the works are conceived in the main thought currents of their respective milieus and vary, therefore, in their emphases from century to century, but it is equally true that they are comparatively free from circumscription of narrow theological concepts lying outside the mainstream of Christian thought. Among the underlying assumptions are these: there is an omnipotent, omniscient, immutable, holy God who ought to be worshiped; man is a depraved creature and, therefore, severed from the divine life; God is merciful and just toward man in extending to him grace through the atonement; man is responsible for his actions and must accept proffered mercy; God is sovereign in all matters.

General acceptance of the tenets of the Christian faith strengthened the devotional tone by diverting the writer from theological disputations and inducing him to give primary attention to the implications of righteous principle for pious living. The devotional writer is not indifferent to doctrine, for acceptance of sound belief is everywhere the solid foundation upon which he builds. But the worshipful tone dominant in his writings is aided where argument gives way to a discussion of man's duties that are attendant upon a sovereign God whose pattern man seeks to emulate.

One looks even further than spiritual tone for distinguishing features of early devotional prose. A critical examination of the great devotional writers reveals dominant themes that occur repeatedly. These include (1) preoccupation with the Scriptures and Christ as the basis and model for perfection in this life, (2) emphasis upon self-renunciation, (3) injunctions to prayer and meditation, (4) desire for union with God, and (5) ways and means of implementing doctrine in practical affairs. It is by treating these themes that Law establishes himself firmly in the devotional tradition.[7]

II Christian Perfection *and* A Serious Call

Written at approximately the same time in Law's career, *Christian Perfection* and *A Serious Call to a Devout and Holy Life* are very similar in content and purpose, so that many of the generalizations made about one apply equally to the other. The first insists that the nature and design of Christianity is to deliver us from the misery and disorder of our present state and to raise us to an enjoyment of the divine nature. Law defines Christian perfection as the "holy and religious conduct of ourselves in every state of life." Such a life involves more than performing a set of duties or withdrawing to a cloister; rather it is a change of nature, a new life perfectly devoted to God. It requires renunciation of the world and stringent self-denial to prepare the way for divine grace to permeate the inner life. All sinful practices are to be eschewed and the life given to a constant state of devotion and imitation of the life of Christ.

A Serious Call also insists upon true devotion as a life given entirely to God rather than merely performing isolated acts of worship. It views shortcomings in devotion as resulting more from a paralysis of intention than from inadvertent failures in pious deportment. It offers practical counsel freely for the handling of worldly goods. Holiness of life is said to belong to all ranks and provides the greatest peace and happiness known in this world. But

misery, sensuality, and spiritual emptiness follow naturally in the
wake of religious neglect. Specific counsel for righteous living
includes special hours for prayer, practice of humility, and reading of
edifying books. The excellence of the truly devout spirit is illustrated
in numerous character portraits.

That both of these treatises were essentially books of devotion was
recognized by many of Law's contemporaries. Bishop Wilson said,
"Law's *Christian Perfection* fell into my hands by Providence, and
after reading it I recommended it so heartily to a friend near London
that he procured eighteen copies for each of our parochial libraries; I
have recommended it to my clergy after the most affecting manner as
the likeliest way to bring them to a most serious temper."[8] The
prefatory advertisement to the 1893 edition states, "The *Christian
Perfection* is the first work of Law's which as a beacon directs the
wayfarer through the straight gate into the narrow way with its
pitfalls and manifold difficulties which he knew so well and along
which he himself had passed."[9] By "pitfalls" and "difficulties" the
writer evidently referred to the spiritual problems that commonly
beset the Christian life. Similarly, Law's biographer points out the
tremendous influence that *A Serious Call* has had as a devotional
guide for important people who fell under its influence and asserts
freely that "whoever sits down without prejudice and attentively
reads it through will rise up the wiser man and better Christian." He
quotes Edward Gibbon, who said, "Mr. Law's master work, the
Serious Call, is still read as a popular and powerful book of
devotion." He also cites Bishop Horne as one who "conformed
himself in many respects to the strictness of Law's rules of devotion."[10]

Inasmuch as Law previously had been occupied with controversial
writing, it may be that he then saw the need for setting forth the
essentials of a true profession of Christianity as a positive antidote for
error. The practical rules which he lays down for achieving perfection
in *Christian Perfection* are very close to the rules allegedly drawn up
by himself when he was at Cambridge:[11]

I. To fix deep in my mind that I have one business upon my hands—to
seek for eternal happiness by doing the will of God.
II. To examine everything that relates to me in this view, as it serves or
obstructs this only end of life.
III. To think nothing great or desirable because the world thinks it so; but
to form all my judgments of things from the infallible Word of God, and
direct my life according to it.

IV. To avoid all concerns with the world, or the ways of it, but where religion and charity oblige me to act.

V. To remember frequently, and impress it upon my mind deeply, that no condition of this life is for enjoyment, but for trial; and that every power, ability, or advantage we have are all so many talents to be accounted for to the Judge of all the world.

VI. That the greatness of human nature consists in doing nothing else but in imitating the Divine nature. That, therefore, all the greatness of this world, which is not in good actions, is perfectly beside the point.

VII. To remember often and seriously how much of time is thrown away, from which I can expect nothing but the charge of guilt; and how little there may be to come on which an eternity depends.

VIII. To avoid all excess in eating and drinking.

IX. To spend as little time as I possibly can among such persons as can receive no benefit from me, nor I from them.

X. To be always fearful of letting my time slip away without some fruit.

XI. To avoid all idleness.

XII. To call to mind the presence of God whenever I find myself under temptation to sin and to have immediate recourse to prayer.

XIII. To think humbly of myself; and with great charity of all others.

XIV. To forbear from all evil speaking.

XV. To think often of the life of Christ, and to propose it as a pattern for myself.

XVI. To pray, privately, thrice a day, besides my morning and evening prayer.

XVII. To keep from [*public houses*] as much as I can without offence.

XVIII. To spend some time in giving an account of the day previous to evening prayer: how have I spent this day? What sin have I committed? What temptations have I withstood? Have I performed all my duty?

III *Traditional Themes: Models for Perfection*

Of the dominant themes that distinguish Law's early writings as devotional, one is preoccupation with the Scriptures and Christ as the basis and model for Christian perfection in this life. This theme points up the "allness" of God and challenges man to emulate the example of perfect virtue if he would attain the spiritual heights of which he is capable. It sees through the vanity of the world, places a premium on the value of eternity, and urges man to take advantage of every aid that will prepare him for life with God. The basis for achieving Christlikeness, which usually consists of accepting provisions of the atonement as described in the Scriptures, is held constantly before the believer.

One may safely assume that Law's ideas on the subject of

perfection were not completely underivative, for striving toward perfection has long been emphasized by those who have incited others to pious living. St. Augustine, a popular, early nonnative devotional writer available to Law in English translation, illustrates well this theme. After a long inner struggle and search of the Scriptures concerning the nature of God, the origin of evil, free will, and rest for the soul, he finally realizes that Deity is unchangeable, that whatever God has made is good and worthy to be praised, and that Jesus Christ is the only mediator between man and his Creator.[12] Another medieval survival of a popular nonnative work which enjoyed great popularity in English translation was Thomas à Kempis's *Imitation of Christ*. As the title suggests, the writer emphasizes that we ought to emulate the Supreme Model of perfection.[13] Law's fondness for à Kempis's admonitions are well known.

Near Law's own time, the righteous François Fenelon, with whose works Law was evidently familiar, also wrote a well-known devotional book on Christian perfection, which may have set Law to thinking on the subject. Deeply moved by the possibility of achieving a state of perfection in this life, Fenelon wrote letters of spiritual counsel and direction to persons living in the late seventeenth century. He dealt with several aspects of the spiritual life which are also handled by Law: use of one's own time, imitation of Christ, knowledge of God, and self-renunciation.[14] Both men depict the same yearning for high spiritual attainment. At approximately the same time, St. Francis de Sales, whom Law also read, wrote *Introduction to the Devout Life* to combat the idea that holiness is possible only for those who live in the seclusion of the cloister. He said, "Wherever we are, we may and ought to aspire to the perfect life." The aim of devotion, he added, does not consist so much in exterior practice as in the interior dispositions of the heart.[15]

Few writers agree completely on what constitutes Christian perfection, although most admit that it is a limited, or relative, perfection—such as may be achieved by man in an imperfect world. Law's early definition, "the right performance of our necessary duties . . . in the holy and righteous conduct of ourselves in every state of life," which agrees essentially with what Walter Hilton taught about four hundred years earlier, envisions an unusually high standard of piety. Man ought to strive for the same perfection that Adam knew before the fall. And to Law, Adamic and angelic perfection were one and the same. Not every writer upon the subject concurs with Law's high standard; nevertheless, underlying each treatment of perfection is a sincere desire to attain by grace and good works a flawless state of personal righteousness.

By "right performance of our necessary duties" Law does not refer merely to ritualistic observances or faithful discharge of good works; neither does he mean withdrawal to places of religious retirement to engage in penance and solitary meditation. ". . . The inward Piety of the Heart and Mind which constitutes the State of Christian Perfection, depends upon no outward Circumstances."[16] Like Francis de Sales, who aimed to show that true devotion consists principally in the interior disposition of the heart, Law also speaks of devotion as "the habit of mind," the inward state of the heart. Again and again Law emphasizes that piety and devotion must involve the totality of one's life before they will be acceptable to God.

In his study of the place of perfection in Christian theology, Robert Flew cites Law as an illustration of those who recalled the Anglican Church to the pursuit of higher objectives than she had sought hitherto. He also tempers his praise for Law by expressing his fear that Law's exacting demands upon conduct may be depressing to the average worshiper, although the ideal held forth is no less attainable than that found in the New Testament.[17]

Those who would place Law outside the mainstream of Christian belief because of what they refer to as "unorthodox views" fail to take into account his clear statements upon key teachings of the Christian church. At no point is he more consonant with the orthodox position than when he depicts scriptural doctrines as the bases for a life of devotion, especially as they apply to the change that must be wrought in man's nature: "All the Precepts and Doctrines of the Gospel are founded on these two great Truths, the deplorable Corruption of human Nature, and its new Birth in Christ Jesus."[18]

Law's devotional predecessors likewise alluded to the Scriptures constantly as the basis for transforming their lives: St. Augustine gave himself to diligent study of the Bible as an antidote to heresy and guide to devotion; Jeremy Taylor speaks of the biblical foundation for holy living and holy dying. Even the mystics of the medieval school constantly refer to the scriptural basis for godliness.

Two Renaissance masters of English prose who also wrote outstanding devotional prose recommending the perfection of life to which every man ought to aspire are John Donne and Jeremy Taylor. Concerned only with his own soul, Donne writes with a psychological intimacy that is unique in the manuals of devotion. The *Devotions*

Upon Emergent Occasions purports to be a collection of twenty-three musings divided into "Meditations," "Expostulations," and "Prayers." There is no single plan; the emergencies of the sickness that has descended upon the writer provide the subjects for meditation. In the following brief selection from "Meditation One" and "Prayer One" the author contemplates the present state of man's existence in this world and recognizes the necessity of God's grace if man would lead a life that would satisfy a righteous standard:

Variable, and therefore miserable condition of man; this minute I am well, and am ill this minute. I am surpriz'd with a sodaine change, and alteration to worse, and can impute it to no cause, nor call it by name. . . . Deliver me, therefore, O my God, from these vaine imaginations; that it is an over curious, a dangerous thing, to come to that tenderness, that rawness, that scrupulousness, to fear every concupiscence, every offer of sin, that this suspicious, and jealous diligence will turn to an inordinate dejection of spirit, and a diffidence in thy care and providence.[19]

Underneath Donne's elaborate style lay a simplicity of religious faith. In the *Devotions* . . . "the menace of death was the signal for the unwrapping of all the faculties of body, mind, and soul in a fervent adoration of God." His spirit and manner portray a heart in earnest to declare allegiance and express gratitude to God for mercy extended to him.

Two contemporary devotional classics recommending the godly life, which were even more suited to the general taste than Donne's, were Jeremy Taylor's *Holy Living* and *Holy Dying*. Taylor states in the dedication of *Holy Living* to Richard Vaughan that he hopes to make readily accessible guides and rules of conduct for all those persons who would bear the character of a true Christian. *Holy Dying*, published in 1651, one year after the publication of *Holy Living*, holds constantly before the reader the "allness" of the Creator. Both works exude the same yearning for pious living, the same reasonable manner through the employment of Scripture and lessons gained from history in inducing man to live a holy life. *Holy Dying* deals with general preparations for death through consideration of the vanity and shortness of life and the need for self-improvement; it considers the state of sickness and the temptation and grace attendant upon it, and the kind of assistance to be given to the dying person by the clergy.

Law is even more emphatic than most of his predecessors in insisting that the "new birth" is not only a personal religious crisis in which one experiences a momentary "change of heart," but a continuing process of moral renovation as well. He reiterates the necessity of man's participating continuously in this redemptive act which will put him in possession of a new life. Even after man possesses the "new birth" he must continue to explore mentally and spiritually its meaning, for "this principle of a new life is the very Essence and Soul of Christianity, it is the Seal of the Promises, the Mark of our Sonship, the Earnest of the Inheritance, the Security of our Hope, and the Foundation of all our Acceptance with God."[20] More than a set of regulations superimposed from without, Christianity involves an entire change of nature and temper—a life perfectly devoted to God. Such a change will stamp the devotional disposition upon one's nature:

When Holiness is such a Habit in our Minds, so directs and forms our Designs, as Covetousness and Ambition directs and governs the Actions of such Men, as are governed by no other Principles, then we are alive in God, and living Members of the mystical Body of his Son Jesus Christ.[21]

Everywhere in *Christian Perfection* and *A Serious Call* the author supplies incentives for living by righteous rule. But he gives no more exalted concept of what a life of devotion really signifies than when he states that all Christians must imitate the life and example of Jesus Christ:

... This is the sole End of all the Counsels, Commands, and Doctrines of Christ, to make us like himself, to fill us with his *Spirit* and *Temper*, and make us live according to the Rule and Manner of his Life.[22]

Law does not mean that conformity to such a high ideal should be reserved for clergymen alone. Persons in all stations of life, including servants, coachmen, and the like, must also follow after perfection. "Learn of me, for I am meek and lowly in heart" applies equally to all. No man may do less than to emulate the supreme example of the Lord, who embodied perfectly every concept of righteousness known to man. Law's religious pronouncements come alive and enhance their democratic appeal as he demonstrates the practicality and feasibility of living in accord with the Divine Example.

When Law makes human perfection consist of likeness to Jesus Christ, he is not only speaking like a traditional churchman, but he is also pointing up a theme that pervades most of the devotional literature of the past. He may have copied the idea from one of the patristic writers from the West such as Ambrose, Jerome, Augustine, or Gregory; or he may have been influenced by one of the late Latin Fathers: Anselm of Canterbury, Bernard of Clairvaux, Thomas Aquinas, and Bonaventura. It was a common practice for English writers on religious subjects to look back to the Fathers for inspiration; however, Law seldom mentions them specifically.

Helen McHugh in her study of early English devotional prose notes that Law's treatment of Christlikeness in *Christian Perfection* does present an interesting parallel to that of one of the most popular medieval devotional works, Nicholas Love's translation of *The Mirrour of the Blessed Lyf of Jesus Christ*. Based on a well-known work by Bonaventura, this work, like Law's *Christian Perfection*, aimed to "stir men's hearts to love God" through emulation of the life of Christ. It urged as a spiritual benefit the contemplation of each phase of the Lord's earthly mission and passion.[23] The more than twenty extant manuscripts testify to the *Mirrour*'s contemporary popularity.

IV   *Self-Renunciation*

A second prominent theme in the literary tradition here explored is that of self-renunciation. If the preceding theme centers on the "allness" of the Creator, the present one emphasizes the "nothingness" of the creature. Man is continually reminded by the devotional writer that he is depraved and therefore unworthy in God's sight. Not only must he admit to a depraved state, but he must follow the steps in self-abnegation adequate to cope with this condition. Renouncing worldly tempers, disdain for self-enjoyment, weaning of the heart from worldly affairs are the disciplines usually enjoined for severing of self from sinful entanglements.

An important early devotional treatise that outlined the religious duties attendant upon acceptance in the St. James order was *The Rule of Anchoresses (Ancren Riwle)*. Directed particularly toward helping nuns (and monks) to live lives of strict piety, *The Rule of Anchoresses* taught that conformity to the principal practices of the church was equated with gaining acceptance with God.[24] Just as monks and nuns must live exemplary lives in communities, so anchoresses and anchorites must lead similar lives alone or in small groups. Emphasis here lay upon "right doing" more than "right being." The anchoress must keep herself like the birds of heaven— unspotted from the world—avoiding the seven deadly sins, shunning all idle talk, abstaining from backbiting, eschewing flattery, resisting gossip, and guarding well her senses, particularly her eyes, which afford the most likely avenue for the entrance of sin to the soul. Originally written by an unknown cleric for the guidance of three young recluse women, *The Rule of Anchoresses* illustrates the work of an artist with a profound knowledge of human life who treats, if severely, with good sense and moderation, several problems of the ascetic life.

Most writers of devotion give considerable space to the discussion of self-denial as a necessary antidote to vainglory and passion. The *Private Devotions of Lancelot Andrewes*, one of the classics of devotion from the Renaissance, is quite explicit in its treatment of self-renunciation through confession of sin and pleas for divine mercy:

But I repent, O Lord, I repent. Help thou mine impenitence, and more and more, pierce, rend, crush my heart. Behold, O Lord, that I am indignant with myself, for my senseless, profitless, hurtful, perilous passions. . . . I humble myself under Thy mighty hand, I bend to Thee, O Lord, my knees, I fall on my face to the earth. . . .[25]

Nothing in the whole range of devotional literature is comparable to Andrewes's emphasis upon self-denial and entreaties for divine aid, and his strong language and "heart-laden" clauses are cast in an unforgettable style.

The rigors of self-renunciation are illustrated further by François Fenelon, who wrote, "Happy the soul which by a severe self-renunciation holds itself ceaselessly in the hands of the Creator, ready to do everything which He wishes, which never stops saying to itself a hundred times a day, 'Lord, what wouldst Thou that I should do?'"[26]

Much earlier, St. Augustine in his devotional *City of God* praised the spiritual benefit of humility and self-renunciation: "In humility, therefore, there is this to be admired, that it elevates the heart; and in pride this, that it dejects it. . . . Godly humility exalts one, in making him God's subject. But pride, the vice, refusing this subjection, falls from Him that is above all."[27] The author of *Theologica Germanica* also states, "Let no one suppose that he may come to the True Light and perfect cognition and to the Christ Life . . . by hearsay or by reading or study. . . . A man will not come to it as long as he at all values anything, or cherishes anything. . . ."[28] Well-worn copies of these works were in Law's library at King's Cliffe.

Although not lacking in democratic appeal, Law gives by far the most space to advising persons of rank as to how they ought to conduct themselves in keeping with their privileges and high stations. The principle of the tithe, or the giving of a tenth of one's earnings to the church, has been followed by churchmen generally as the biblical standard, but the principle that Law invokes goes far beyond the Jewish concept of the tithe. He tells people of means that "the rule of *forgiving* is also the rule of *giving*; you are not to *give*, or do good to *seven*, but to seventy times seven."[29] Proper handling of estates and fortunes, as in the performing of other good works, becomes a concomitant of faith. That Law believed implicitly in this view of Christian stewardship is evident by the systematic, unselfish manner in which he dispensed his own goods in the King's Cliffe community.

Still speaking to persons of leisure, Law states that rest and retirement, in themselves lawful, must also be controlled and directed by hearts filled with devotion. He warns against the gentleman's spending an exorbitant amount of time in sports and a woman's spending much time and money in adorning her own person. Mindful of the eighteenth-century women who gave much attention to ostentatious dress and costly cosmetics, and who thought only of physical comfort, Law presents the characters Flavia and Miranda as contrasts in practical piety. The former, very orthodox in her belief, well-practiced in decrying "heretics and schismatics" and very faithful in her attendance at church, taking the sacrament and other duties is, in most ways, a paragon of virtue. However, Flavia has one flaw: she is more careful about her body than about her soul:

The rising of a *pimple* in her face, the sting of a *gnat*, will make her keep to her room two or three days . . . She never thinks she is well enough . . . It costs her a great deal in *sleeping*-draughts and *waking*-draughts, in *spirits* for the head, in *drops* for the nerves, in *cordials* for the stomach, and in *saffron* for her *tea*.[30]

Miranda, on the other hand, exemplifies the virtues of Christian perfection:

She has but one reason for doing, or not doing, for liking, or not liking anything, and that is, the will of God. She is not so weak as to pretend to add, what is called the *fine lady* to the true Christian. . . . She has but one rule that she observes in her dress, to be always *clean*, and in the *cheapest* things. Everything about her resembles the purity of her soul, and she is always clean without, because she is always pure within.[31]

Following the graphic account of the holy Miranda, Law enjoins persons of her sex to follow her example. He admits that since the beginning of Christianity there have been two principal ranks, one that served God in secular life, and one that renounced the enjoyments of life, as "riches, marriage, honours, and pleasures." Both classes receive the approbation of God, but peculiar favor falls upon Miranda's way of life.[32]

One easily detects in Law's directives biographical overtones. He rigorously applied to himself the precepts he enjoined upon others. Law's setting apart nine o'clock each morning for the consideration of humility indicates the importance he attached to that virtue.

Paternus, another character portrait in *A Serious Call*, is exhorted to shun "strife, or envy, or emulation, or vainglory." Through Flautus, the searcher after happiness, who flits from one project to another and who delights himself alternately with fine clothing, gaming, the diversions of the town, drinking, breeding and educating dogs, architecture, travel, education, and dieting, Law decries the pride of the day.[33]

Underneath Law's emphasis upon "selling" and "giving to the poor" lies his utter disdain for self-enjoyment. To him, the Christian could pursue godliness only by resisting temptations to worldly pleasure, even though they may appear harmless. The rich are naturally susceptible to powerful temptations to lavish upon themselves worldly goods which may distract from the worship of God. The goods themselves may be harmless, but they easily lure the worshiper from the main business of loving God with "all his heart, mind, and strength." Self must be curbed, for it is the center of all unholy desires. Law makes much of the careful disposition of one's possessions, for he feels that they offer to man the most common temptations. Ridding oneself completely of earthly goods is the most sure way of averting temptation. A right motive for self-renunciation is important also to produce a spiritual effect upon the worshiper:

... This Renunciation of the World, which is thought too great an Extreme, to be taken from the Command given to the young Man in the Gospel, is the Common Temper of Christianity, and a Doctrine the most universally taught of any other. It is indeed the very Heart and Soul of Christian Piety, it is the natural Soil, the proper Stock from whence all the Graces of a Christian naturally grow forth, it is a Disposition of all others the most necessary and most productive of Virtue.[34]

Contrary to the common view that a life of self-renunciation leads to unhappiness, Law points out that whatever happiness we know in the world is brought about through religion: "Why may not poor People give themselves up to *Discontent*, to *Impatience* and *Repining*? Is it not because Christianity requires the same Virtue in all States of life? Is it not because the Rewards of Religion are sufficient to make us thankful in every Condition?" Again, "If therefore we are to love God with all our Heart and with all our Soul, it is absolutely necessary, that we be first persuaded, that we have no Happiness but in Him alone, and that we are capable of no other good, but what arises from enjoyment of the Divine Nature."[35]

Of course Law recognizes the limitations of joys in the present world, for he believes that imperfections in both man and nature accrue from the fall. But for the pious heart, happiness extends beyond the temporal world. In fact, happiness here may be subject to accidents of time and place, but these are more than compensated for by the anticipation of permanent joys of the future life:

There are many Things in human Life, which it would be in vain for you to aspire after, but the Happiness of the next, which is the Sum of all Happiness, is secure and safe to you against all Accidents.[36]

Although Law and John Wesley were contemporaries who were occupied by similar religious interests, each appealed to a different class of people and strove for different immediate goals. Whereas the work of Wesley was primarily to awaken the lower classes to their need of religion, the divine commission of Law was to take already converted men of the educated and intellectual class and challenge them to a more consecrated life. Even so, Law did not modify his Christian precepts to suit the tastes of the educated group: "He represented to a generation who worshiped the golden mean the uncompromising character of Christianity, and must have taught some among them how much more practical an ideal we can set before ourselves when we strive after perfection than when we aim at decency."[37]

In keeping with the devotional theme of self-renunciation, but illustrating more particularly the practical advice that Law offers to those who would lead lives of piety, are his pronouncements upon attending the stage and reading "vain and impertinent books." Law contends that stage entertainment is a "corrupt and sinful Entertainment, contrary to the whole Nature of Christian Piety, and constantly to be avoided by all sincere Christians." His tone is more denunciatory and unequivocal than that of Jeremy Collier's earlier and better-known essay on the stage. When asked whether it is unlawful for a Christian to go to the playhouse, he answers, ". . . It is absolutely unlawful—as unlawful as for a Christian to be a *Drunkard* or a *Glutton*, or to *Curse* and *Swear*."[38]

Law makes no attempt to discriminate between good and bad plays; he condemns categorically. The actors are profane, passionate, and immodest; the subjects which these actors depict are ribald and impure; the effect produced upon the playgoers is essentially evil. The conscientious Christian steward, therefore, cannot pay his money for such a wicked business. Law concludes:

An Entertainment therefore which applies to the Corruption of our Nature, which awakens our disordered Passions, and teaches to relish lewdness, immoral Rant, and Profaneness, is exceedingly sinful, not only as it is a Breach of some particular Duty, but as it contradicts the *whole Nature*, and opposes *every Part* of our Religion.[39]

To those who spoke of the stage as a "harmless diversion," Law declares it as contrary to the whole nature of religion as the worship of images. Playgoing is more than an *occasion* for sinning; it is by its *nature* grossly sinful, like lewdness, lying, and profanity. The modern reader has little sympathy for Law's extreme Puritan bias, but in his day opinions of the stage differed widely. At least one prominent spokesman, John Dennis, responded to Law with a spirited defense of the stage.[40]

Law's failure to appreciate drama as a faithful portrayal and criticism of life is not so unusual when we remember that plays and playgoing were generally unpopular among the churchmen of that time. Audiences were noisy and desirous of sensational entertainment. And Law, rather than damning everyone who attended a play, appeals to the expediency of the practice for one who would live a life of devotion. As he explains, "It ought not to be concluded, that because I affirm the *Playhouse* to be an Entertainment *contrary* to Modesty, that therefore I accuse all People as void of Modesty, who ever go to it."[41] But the pious person ought to consider the wisdom of attending the theater,

. . . whether it hinders or in any way affects that Spirit and Temper, which all . . . Devotions aspire after. Is it conformable to that Heavenly affection, that Love of God, that Purity of Heart, that Wisdom of Mind, that Perfection of Holiness, that Contempt of the World, that Watchfulness and

Self-denial, that Humility and Fear of Sin? Is it conformable to these Graces, which are to be the daily *Subject* of all . . . prayers?[42]

Law makes plain his attitude toward reading and the general education of youth when he states in *Christian Perfection* that the reading of "vain and impertinent books" is inimical to the devotional life. Specifically, he mentions "Books of *Wit* and *Humour, Romances, Plays*, and other Productions of the Poets" as particularly offensive to the Christian. It is principally this view that elicits frequent criticisms of *Christian Perfection*: (1) that it crusades against all kinds of human learning, (2) that it is a melancholy book. The modern reader may be inclined to agree that Law is at times over-distrustful of man's ability to choose for himself what he ought or ought not to read. His injunction to put aside all unedifying books seems to place an unwarranted premium upon innocence. His growing aversion to secular reading may account in part for his mounting failure to allude to his readings in the classics.

It is easy, however, to misjudge Law when he advises against the reading of any book "that does not *edify* and minister Grace to the Hearers. . . ." Although the typical eighteenth-century attitude toward art was that it ought to instruct, Law carried that view to the extreme. When he singled out the types of books that he believed to be injurious to the devotional life, he referred to most secular literature, including poetry, plays, and French romances, which constituted the popular reading for the leisure class. Although severe in manner, Law's disapproval of such reading was shared by many Nonconformists of his day, as well as by conservative-minded adherents of the Established Church.

One must remember, too, that the author is trying to safeguard a life of devotion. *Christian Perfection* and *A Serious Call* become devotional treatises because the sole intent of their author is to aid the Christian in fashioning his life to gain divine approval. Admittedly, Law's religious outlook was narrow; flexibility was not one of his virtues. His greatest fault, however, may be merely overcaution in spiritual matters. He believed that the end of life is the vision of God, which implies, as Kenneth Kirk points out, "that the highest prerogative of the Christian in this life as well as hereafter is the activity of worship." If one grants this premise, the practical corollary follows that "the principal duty of the Christian moralist is to stimulate the spirit of worship in those to whom he addresses himself."[43] And if, as Kirk avers further, Christianity came into a world contending that some men at least had seen God and had found in the vision the sum of human happiness, and "worship is the best way to lift the soul out of its preoccupation with itself" to center its aspirations on God, then Law conformed admirably to this ideal. His austere opinions of what a Christian ought to read and where he ought to go may be interpreted as efforts to eliminate every distraction from worship.

If one wonders whether the offering of practical advice is germane to a literature that usually emphasizes the meditative aspects of worship, he can quickly discover precedents in early devotional literature. The anchoress in *Ancren Riwle* was to emulate the birds of heaven. She should shun idle talk, keep silent at meals, and eschew flattery. Jeremy Taylor speaks at length about the course of the Christian in the practice of Christian justice: he should obey human laws, pay reverence to his ruler, provide for his children's education and employment, use few words in bargaining, and give alms to the poor.[44] Arthur Dent in his popular Renaissance religious guide insists that all men are to be employed for the benefit of the church or commonwealth by relieving the poor or performing other helpful service.[45] Law's advice concerning unedifying books and the stage, therefore, corresponds to other practical counsel offered by devotionalists before him.

Although Law attempts to be "reasonable" in offering practical advice, he is less convincing when he talks about the stage and the reading of books than when he comments upon other related subjects. For instance, he is much less extreme, if not more logical, when he insists that charity must follow faith as the "ornament of behavior" just as love and tenderness for mankind must supplant hate:

Charity, Chastity, Sobriety, and Justice, may be practised without Christian Piety: a *Jew*, a *Heathen*, may be charitable and temperate; but to make these Virtues become Parts of Christian Piety, they must proceed from a Heart *truly* turned unto God, that is full of an *infant* Simplicity, that is *crucified* with Christ, that is *born* again of the Spirit, that has overcome the *World*.[46]

This manifestation of intense spirituality in the overt acts of the everyday life of a Christian bears out Helen White's comment upon the Tudor devotional literature of an earlier century: "Even in this very inward matter of devotion there is always a certain practicality, a focusing of action, highly characteristic of the temper of popular religion. . . ."[47]

V *Injunctions to Prayer*

When one remembers that "the goal of all prayer is communion
with . . . Divinity"—that "in all traditions men have believed that in
prayer man enters into the presence of God"—one understands why
the prayer theme assumes such a prominent place in devotional
literature. The discussion of motives for prayer and how a constant
state of prayer may be maintained, observation of set times for
prayer, composing prayers for special occasions, learning how to
pray—all combine in varying degrees to constitute a theme that is
germane to that great body of literature recommending pious living.

Among early specialized books dealing with formal helps to prayer
which exerted a marked influence upon the English mind in the
turbulent sixteenth century were the two Edwardian books of 1549
and 1552. The Psalter and its offshoot, the Primer, also served as
basic service books of the church, as well as furnishing source books
for private devotion. Elizabethan zest for guides to godliness is
further seen in collections of prayers and printed selections from the
Scriptures as directives for prayer. Speaking of the widespread
appeal that these books had for the layman, Louis B. Wright states,
"With a book to tell him of doctrine and the means of knowing his
state of salvation with a manual of biblical interpretation and a
handbook of meditations and prayers, any apprentice or tradesman
could deal with God for his soul."[48]

During this same period at least three important continental
imports from Catholic countries also made deep impressions upon
English readers. The first of these, which focused upon the centrality
of prayer in the devotional life, was Fray Luis de Granada's *Book of
Prayer and Meditation*, published in Spain in 1554 and passing
through ten London editions by 1663. *Spiritual Combat* by the
Italian Lorenzo Scupoli, published in English in Louvain in 1598,
and François de Sales's *Introduction to the Devout Life* not only
illustrate the same emphasis, but also reveal the English reader's
inclination to read devotional literature from Catholic sources.[49]

One of the most widely read devotional writers of the Elizabethan
period was Thomas Becon, whose *Flower of Godly Prayers, Pathway
Unto Prayer*, and *Pomander of Prayer* further illustrate the centrality
of the prayer theme. *Flower of Godly Prayers* treats of prayers for
special occasions—mealtimes, for example—and special people:
kings, judges, magistrates, soldiers, mariners, and the like.[50] Becon's
Pathway Unto Prayer lists several steps toward effective prayer for

the soul which seeks to achieve a worshipful attitude: understanding what prayer is, preparing one's own heart for prayer, considering the proper place, subject, and time for prayer. Becon's detailed description of this carefully planned approach to God also speaks of right motive as essential to the strengthening of the devout life.

The impulse for improvement of men in both low and high stations may be seen in the *Pomander of Prayer*, which passed through six editions between 1558 and 1578. Dedicating it to Anne of Cleves, Becon says, "I thought it good to give unto you this my Pomander of Prayer, wherein are briefly contained such godly prayers as are most meet in this our age to be used of all degrees and estates. . . ."[51] Here again are listed prayers for spiritual gifts, for certain times of the day and for special occasions, as well as private prayers to be said by all classes of people.

Although the traditional conception of devotional activity held in the Middle Ages and for about one hundred years afterward was prayer, and subsequent periods witnessed a broadening of that devotional concept to include the general welfare of the Christian life, the stress upon prayer as a valid Christian duty did not diminish, as is shown in the versatile handling of the subject by Richard Baxter and Lancelot Andrewes, two popular seventeenth-century clergymen. Baxter dwelt at length upon "heavenly contemplation" as the supreme joy of earth and prayer as the chief means for attaining it.[52] The *Private Devotions* of Andrewes belongs to an older form which was a favorite with English writers—manuals of prayers for each day of the week. Composed for private use and published almost fifty years after the author's death, the *Devotions* followed the plan of setting down each scriptural verse or clause which had a personal significance; in so doing, as Alexander Whyte suggests, Andrewes anticipated and "fulfilled all William Law's best counsels."

Whether one is reading the formal prayer directives of a Primer or the more personal accounts of St. Paul or St. Augustine, one sees that the various writers, even though they vary in their emphases, are in essential agreement upon their spiritual counsels for prayer. Whether it is St. Augustine praising the Triune God with "integrations of Platonic speculation" or Bernard of Clairvaux "warming his asceticism with the glow of Divine Humanity and tenderness for the Virgin-Mother," it is man praying to the same God in a universal language which one age understands quite as well as another.

Law dwells at length upon the theme of prayer in both of the early devotional treatises, with slight variations of emphases. In *Christian*

Perfection he departs from the more conventional practice of specifying certain times and specialized forms of prayer. Consistent with his previous definition of devotion, he contends, "External Acts of Devotion are, like other external Actions, very liable to Falseness, and are only so far good and valuable as they proceed from a right Disposition of heart and mind."[53] It is not that Law discounts completely the ritual of prayer, although he contends that no single religious performance supplies full proof that a life is holy. Law's attitude toward forms of prayer in *A Serious Call* sounds much more like that of a member of the Church of England than in *Christian Perfection*:

For though I think a form of prayer very *necessary* and *expedient* for *public* worship, yet if anyone can find a better way of raising his heart unto God in private, than by *prepared forms* of prayer, I have nothing to object against it. . . .

. . . I believe . . . that the *generality* of Christians ought to use *forms* of prayer, at all the regular times of prayer. It seems right for everyone to begin with a *form* of prayer. . . .[54]

The form is meant to be only a discipline to start the soul along the road of pious thought and meditation. But as the concentration of spirit leads toward the inner vision, the worshiper may leave his man-made aids behind. Law states it thus: "If in the midst of his devotions, he finds his heart ready to break forth into new and higher strains of devotion, he should leave his *form* for awhile and follow those fervours of his heart, till it again wants the assistance of his usual petition."

Law concurs with the leading devotionalists of the past who contend that prayer "is the noblest exercise of the soul, the most exalted use of our best faculties, and the highest imitation of the blessed inhabitants of heaven."[55] Quite in keeping with his devotional forerunners, he makes the Bible and church history the bases for his admonitions:

If our blessed Lord used to pray early before day . . . if the devout *Anna* was day and night in the temple; if St. *Paul* and *Silas* at midnight sang praises unto God; if the *primitive Christians*, for several hundred years, besides their hours of prayer in the day-time, met publicly in the Churches at *mid-night*, to join in Psalms and Prayers, is it not certain that these practices showed the *state* of their heart?[56]

Even as "their way of life was a demonstration of their devotion, so a contrary way of life is a strong proof of a want of devotion." Nevertheless, the author refuses to take the arbitrary position that something is true simply because it is scriptural; rather he prefers to contend for the sweet reasonableness of such a position. If the apostles and saints of the primitive church sensed their need of definite spiritual exercise, so every man who has set for himself high spiritual goals should emulate their examples.

Law's practical treatment of prayer may be seen in his directives for coming into the presence of God: "The first thing you are to do, when you are upon your *knees*, is to shut your *eyes*, and with a short *silence* let your soul place itself in the presence of God. . . ."[57] The time of quiet serves to counter the impatience of the heart as well as to wean it from the unholy, foolish thoughts that frequently fill it. The next step is to use "various expressions of the attributes of God" as may make one "sensible of the greatness and power of the Divine nature." Law becomes explicit:

Begin therefore in words like these: "O Being of all beings, Fountain of all light and glory, gracious Father of men and angels, whose universal Spirit is everywhere present, giving life, and light, and joy, to all angels in heaven, and all creatures upon earth . . ."

[Or] . . . "O Savior of the world, God of God, Light of Light; thou that art the Brightness of thy Father's Glory, and the express Image of his Person; thou that art the Alpha and Omega, the Beginning and End of all things . . ."[58]

Words have a way of speaking to the soul. Although the prayer does not consist merely of fine words, yet the words that refer to God in such an exalted manner and that "most fully express the power and presence of God" serve to stimulate edifying thoughts.

Pursuing the subject of how to pray, Law sets forth the spiritual benefits of singing Psalms in one's private devotions. By singing he means chanting in the manner frequently done in the Church of England according to the *Book of Common Prayer*. Law was a lover of singing and frequently enjoined upon others the need for mastering the rudimentary principles of music so as to allow at least elementary proficiency in singing for one's own edification. Within easy reach of every devotee of worship, however, is the natural change of the voice required for chanting a Psalm.

Singing the Psalms is in keeping with the note of praise that Law recommends as fitting for early morning devotion to awaken the holy impulses and to set the worshiper in good spiritual posture:

. . . Nothing . . . so clears a way for your prayers, nothing . . . so disperses the *dulness* of heart, nothing . . . so purifies the soul from *poor* and *little* passions, nothing . . . so *opens* heaven, or carries your heart so near it, as these *songs* of *praise.*[59]

The Psalms of praise kindle a "holy flame," turn the heart into an altar, and prayers into an incense of worship.

Law's biographer John Overton notes that Law devotes more than twenty-five pages to the subject of Psalm-singing. However, Law was no innovator here; Psalm-singing has long been practiced in the church. Not only did Lancelot Andrewes and Jeremy Taylor make a place for it in their devotional writings, but singing as a source of edification goes back at least as far as Paul and Silas, who sang praises to God in prison, or even to Moses, who sang after being delivered from the Red Sea.

The final observation to be made upon Law's treatment of the devotional theme of prayer in *A Serious Call*, which differs somewhat from his handling in *Christian Perfection*, is his call to special times of prayer throughout the day to maintain at all times the white heat of devotion. Such observation of set times for prayer is a commonplace in devotional literature. Jeremy Taylor composed prayers to be said as one dresses in the morning, at evening, and before retiring. Thomas Becon similarly listed prayers for different hours of the day. Caroline divines made much of the Prayer Book pattern of special hours for prayers. Law did not integrate the Prayer Book practice into his recommendations, but following, as Overton suggests, the canonical hours of the church, he notes even the themes that are appropriate for the specified times: Six o'clock affords a logical time for thanksgiving and oblation of oneself to God. Nine o'clock in the morning is recommended as a perfect hour for considering humility; twelve o'clock for "universal love," or intercession with God for one's fellow creatures. Devotion at three o'clock should take as its theme resignation. By this time of day the human heart is likely to have been diverted from its central purpose of conforming to the will of God.

The final hour of prayer, six o'clock, is reserved for self-examination—a reconsideration of the "just horror and dread of all sin." Stressing the proneness of all men to depart from goodness, Law enjoins everyone as an antidote to self-will to ponder systematically the following truths:

. . . That the Son of God was forced to become man, to be partaker of all our infirmities, to undergo a poor, painful, miserable, and contemptible life . . .

That all the bloody sacrifices and atonements of the *Jewish* Law were to represent the necessity of this *great sacrifice* . . . That the world is still under the *curse* of sin . . . that all the sons of *Adam* are to go through a painful, sickly life, denying and mortifying their natural appetites . . . that all their penances and self-denials, all their tears and repentance, are only made available by that great Intercession, which is still making for them at the right hand of God.[60]

Law adds that "serious and frequent reflections upon these things" will tend to humble us in our sight and "make us very apprehensive of our own guilt" and therefore more reluctant to censure other people.

Very briefly Law touches upon a fitting meditation prior to going to bed. Here he urges the worshiper to think of the bed as symbolic of the grave, and sleep as death. Reminiscent of John Donne in *Devotions Upon Emergent Occasions*, as the pious man approaches his nightly rest, he may commit himself to sleep as into the hands of God. Since death is an approaching reality, the nightly visitations of sleep will furnish regular reminders of the inevitable severance from life which awaits each one and will thus close the waking day with a meditation centering upon passage out of the temporal world.

Law's stress upon frequency, continuance, and importunity in prayer exhibits further his knowledge that successful spiritual living must pit pious rule against the subtle resistance that lodges in the worshiper. His keen perception of the indisposition and trickery of the heart has been referred to as his "markedly robust and masculine . . . habit of mind and way of looking at matters."[61]

VI   *Union with God*

The popular union-with-God theme, which appears prominently in Law's later works, also receives full treatment in the early devotional treatises:

Would we therefore know our true Rank and Condition, and what Place we belong to, in the Order of Beings, we must search after a *Life that is hid with Christ in God*. We must consider ourselves as Parts of Christ's mystical Body, and as Members of a Kingdom of Heaven.[62]

Some studies have dwelt at length upon the characteristics of his thought after he had assimilated the mystical teachings without acknowledging the unity that underlies all of his writings. Admittedly, the emphasis shifts between the earlier and later works. But that Law believes in and enjoins upon others a unitive experience with God in both religious phases of his life is unmistakable and reveals more continuity of thought than change.

St. Augustine's *Confessions*, which has been called "the first example of true Christian introspection," looked within for the "road map" of the soul's journey toward God. Concerned not merely with the journey, Augustine envisioned a goal to be reached and a truth to be found which were both winsome and fulfilling. He invited God to penetrate his innermost being to inhabit the place formerly occupied by self. His mystical intimacy is indicated in the following passage:

... There is something of a man which neither the spirit of man that is in him, itself knoweth. But Thou, Lord, knowest all of him, Who hast made him. Yet I, though in Thy sight I despise myself, and account myself dust and ashes; yet know I something of Thee, which I know not of myself. . . .
... When I love my God . . . I love a kind of light and melody, and fragrance, and meat, and embracement . . . of my inner man.[63]

Learning in the Middle Ages did not spend itself entirely on biblical exegesis or theological formularies; it also had a penchant for warm devotional prose stressing the union-with-God theme. Four hundred surviving manuscripts reveal the ardent, humanizing manner of Richard Rolle and his descriptions of intimacies with God. Thomas à Kempis also stresses the importance of attending to the "kingdom of God" within. The crowning act in the quest for perfection is to rest in God:

Above all things, and in all things, O my soul, thou shalt rest in the Lord always, for He himself is the everlasting Rest of the Saints.[64]

Law's knowledge of and fondness for the subject of union with God may be seen in his early reading of not only the Church Fathers and medieval mystics, but also Nicholas Malebranche. While Law was at the university, he wrote a thesis on this seventeenth-century metaphysician and absorbed his teachings. Malebranche used Descartes's ontological proof on the necessity of the existence of God. The only world we know is an intelligible world—the world of our ideas. Since ideas have an eternal, infinite character that is independent of our conception, they must be features of an intelligible extension, which has its locus in God. Malebranche taught that "not only do we see all things in God, but in a sense all things are in God." He himself described his philosophy as a commentary on St. Paul's text, "In Him we live, and move, and have our being," and taught that the mind which would know God to a certain degree must be of the same quality as God himself if the two were to become one.[65]

England may have produced her share of mystics, but nonnative writers also achieved great popularity on English soil. Dionysius the Areopagite (ca. 500), Jan Van Ruysbroeck (1293–1381), Meister Eckhart (1260?–1328?), the author of *Theologia Germanica* (ca. 1300), and Jacob Boehme (1575–1624) also manifested divine awareness by setting forth the ecstatic way by which one climbs to oneness with God. The kinship of William Law with the writers of devotional literature is seen nowhere more clearly than in his mystical predilections, and his debt to the mystical school is considerable, as we shall see.

VII *Implementing Doctrine*

Another prominent theme of the early writings of devotional literature, which may at first appear inconsistent with the subjective emphasis already described, is the discussion of ways and means for implementing Christian doctrine in the practical situations of everyday life. While a few writers in the devotional tradition, particularly those of the medieval period, dealt with purely ascetic problems, they constitute the exceptions to standard practice. In most instances, the preoccupations of the devotional writers, in spite of their cultivation of the inner life, are with the day-to-day affairs of laymen living ordinary lives in a practical world.

Of course, the main business of man on this earth is to advance the Kingdom of God; hence man's practical concerns touch primarily the moral relationship with the world about him: How may he better social conditions in the community? How may he practice Christian charity? How may he practice virtue as a civil or religious leader? What books should he read? Contrary to the opinion of many, the devotional writer is no dreamer who withdraws from the world to practice his piety in solitude; rather, there is a certain robustness about his writings which testifies to his social consciousness and practical concern, in spite of the accent upon cultivating the inner life.

This interest in practical affairs may be illustrated among numerous writers. Francis de Sales, who has at heart the spiritual interests of the higher classes particularly, also performs his ministrations to the poor and needy of his time. François Fenelon, though an Archbishop of Cambria with great prestige in court circles, never forgets the needs of the poor peasants. Jeremy Taylor, with all his anticipation of bliss in a future life, advocates grace in the exercise of Christian justice, giving alms as a boon to the needy, and exercising restraint and displaying prudence in his practical advice to heads of families on ways and means of cementing home ties. Arthur Dent also illustrates the practical terms in which these works were conceived when he says:

God doth allowe none to live Idely; but all both great and small, are to be employed one way or another: either for the benefite of the Churche, or Commonwealth: for the good government of their owne households or for the good of Townes and Parishes, and those amongst whome they do converse: or for the succour and reliefe of the poore: or for the furtherance of the Gospell, and the maintenance of the Ministry: or for one good use or another.[66]

Similarly, Law was no idle dreamer. He constantly insisted that faith should be translated into practice—that Christian profession must be matched by practical concerns. Throughout his devotional writing, as in his life, he strove to maintain this balance.

VIII   *Rigorous Stewardship*

Writers of devotional literature are concerned characteristically with translating Christian precepts into practice, but few of them have been more severe than William Law. As Leslie Stephen comments, "Here . . . we are face to face with a man who believes what he says, who is fighting for what he loves and striking at the heart instead of going through the dumb show of argument. . . ."[67] Law was a confirmed Non-juror, but even more he possessed strong convictions about many things which prompted him to act as his conscience directed. Severe probing of Christian motive frequently marks the manner of *Christian Perfection* and *A Serious Call*:

You see two persons, one is regular in *public* and *private* Prayer, the other is not. Now the reason of this difference is not this, that one has *strength* and *power* to observe prayer, and the other has not; but the reason is this, that one *intends* to *please* God in the *duties* of Devotion, and the other has no intention about it. Now the case is the same, in the right or wrong use of our *time* and *money*. You see one person throwing away his time in *sleep* and *idleness*, in *visiting* and *diversions*, and his money in the most vain and unreasonable expenses. You see another careful of every day, dividing his hours by rules of Reason and Religion, and spending all his money in works of charity; now the difference is not owing to this, that one has strength and power to do thus, and the other has not; but it is owing to this, that one *intends to please God* in the right use of all his *time*, and all his *money*, and the other has no intention about it.[68]

Words like these were bound to jar men out of their complacency. Worshipers were used to being told how they might approach God with assurance when they had sinned, or how they might prepare themselves to receive the favor of a merciful God. But seldom was failure in devotion attributed to the apathy of the will. Stripping the heart of every shred of self-righteous attire through impugning of motive exposed shortcomings in the most devout.

The rather severe, denunciatory manner of such passages in *A Serious Call* may lead some reader to think mistakenly that they are religious rantings by a frustrated preacher more than constructive helps to the pious. Law's purpose everywhere, however, is to lead toward a worship that is genuine. But first he spells out clearly that devotion is more than any single act of reverence; it is the set of the soul, the direction of the whole life. Law does not say that *what* one does is unimportant, but he does insist that until the wellspring of the soul is pure, the stream of righteousness proceeding from it is bound to be contaminated. Pleasing God, therefore, must stem from a life that subscribes to righteous duty in every way.

Perhaps a reason why *A Serious Call* and *Christian Perfection* are occasionally referred to as "practical treatises on religion" or books of "hortatory theology" rather than devotional guides is that they are much more analytical, discursive, and hortatory in their appeal than early devotional works which touched more directly upon reflection and pious meditation. Louis Martz points to a "meditative tradition" which flourished both on the continent and in England in the sixteenth and seventeenth centuries. He traces the development of all kinds of spiritual exercises from the early Fathers of the Church through Spain's Fray Luis de Granada's *Book of Prayer and Meditation*; Francis de Sales's *Introduction to the Devout Life; Meditation on the Life of Christ*, attributed to St. Bonaventura; also numerous English writers, beginning with the poet Robert Southwell. He concludes that in many of the major works surveyed the art of meditation is clearly manifested.[69]

While it is true that the treatment of meditation and contemplation is prominent in such well-known devotional prose as Thomas Aquinas's "Of the Contemplative Life" from *Summa Theologica*, Thomas More's *A Godly Meditation*, and Joseph Hall's *Meditations*, Law in form and emphasis differed somewhat from the meditative tradition which Martz defines. Law accepted meditation as an aid to piety, but he did not consider it more important than obeying the many rules that govern the spiritual life. In fact, Law refused to equate devotion with any single act of worship. Devotion meant the dedication and exercise of the whole life to God. In his own way, just as surely as the advocates of meditation and contemplation, he strove to increase the piety of the worshiper.

Richard Baxter or St. Augustine or Thomas Becon was never more in earnest about religion than William Law. One cannot turn to *A Serious Call* or *Christian Perfection* without sensing the fervor and pious impulse which impart a devotional tone to each. That the thought everywhere is suffused with righteous intention can hardly be missed even by the half-perceptive reader.

As one discerns from a review of his early theological and controversial works, as well as from the devotional works themselves, Law conformed closely to the beliefs of the Established Church. The "essential beliefs" of the Anglican Church usually refer to (1) the Being and Nature of God; (2) the Bible and the Creeds; (3) the Church; (4) the Sacraments; (5) Baptism; (6) Holy Communion; (7) the five commonly called sacraments: confirmation, penance, holy orders, holy matrimony, unction; (8) Eschatology; (9) the scheme of Salvation; and (10) the Church and the world. One may encounter occasional criticism of Law's alleged deviations from accepted beliefs, but further examination of the "deviations" usually proves them to be slight. Indeed they do not mar the devotional appeal of the books. One feels that the theological assumptions that underlie Law's early works fall well within the boundaries of accepted Christian belief and that his uppermost thought and purpose are to lead the worshiper into a closer relationship with God as the highest experience of which he is capable in this life.

The *Serious Call* concludes with a recommendation of life governed by devotion. The author recapitulates several points he has made in the treatise:

A devout man makes a true use of his reason; he sees through the *vanity* of the world, discovers the *corruption* of his nature, and the *blindness* of his passions. He lives by a *law* which is not visible to *vulgar eyes*; he enters into a world of *spirits*; he compares the greatest things, sets *eternity* against *time*; and chooses rather to be for ever great in the presence of God when he dies, than to have the greatest share of worldly pleasure while he lives.[70]

Such a station in life is an exalted one. Far from the common opinion that devotion is for little minds, Law praises it as "the greatest sign of a great and noble genius." "He that is devout is full of . . . great thoughts." In one of his rare references to the philosophers he makes the claim that even the "greatest spirits of the heathen world, such as *Pythagoras, Socrates, Plato, Epictetus, Marcus Antonius* . . . owed all their *greatness* to the spirit of devotion." As he says, they were full of God, and their contemplations helped to deliver them from the world's vanity and slavery to bodily passions that they might act as spirits who came from God and who would return to Him. The final evaluation of those who live in accord with these precepts is, according to Law, higher than those who are "bold and daring in the fire of battle."[71]

The salutary effect of Law's early teachings upon the newly formed Evangelical Movement has never been disputed, but the devotional impact of *Christian Perfection* and *A Serious Call* upon other areas of the spiritual life of England—particularly the Established Church—has not always been recognized. Law's strict teachings and inflexible demands probably found little favor among those who preferred a more tolerant religion. Biographer Christopher Walton tells us, however, that Law was consulted by many serious persons as a kind of oracle or spiritual director; Law's letters of spiritual advice to inquiring worshipers may still be read as corroboration of that claim. Although he seldom made a specific reference to the Church of England, he nevertheless addressed his devotional advice to both priests and laymen who fell short of their spiritual ideal. Such writers as G.G. Perry aver that "the church of England owes a great debt to William Law" and that *A Serious Call* and *Christian Perfection* served as "a saving of religion in the land."[72]

Law's supreme passion was to increase the devotion of his hearers. As Gibbon said of him, "If he finds a spark of piety in his reader's mind, he will soon kindle it to a flame."[73] He possessed definite views of man and his place in the world and did not hesitate to urge those views upon all professing Christians. Sometimes this urgency sinks beneath the surface of the writings; again it rises to bold argument.

Readers of devotional literature who are accustomed more to the reflective mood and mild manner of Meister Eckhart, Francis de Sales, or the author of *Theologia Germanica* may be startled at first by the pointed, probing manner of *Christian Perfection* and *A Serious Call*. But devotional literature has many moods. Law's relentless pounding of man's depraved condition, his urgent appeals to the worshiper to flee to divine grace as the only recourse open to him, and his severe probing of Christian motive underline his determination to break through all spiritual apathy to stir the mind and will toward religion. To achieve these aims, he could hardly be mild-mannered and reflective.

Devout souls like William Law demand attention in any age, but in the eighteenth century, marked by its toleration and religious indulgence, his candid view of man's depraved state was particularly striking. Honest recognition of human depravity he regarded as another important step preliminary to a life of devotion:

If we see ourselves in this true Light, we shall see the whole Reason of Christian Self-denial, of Meekness, and Poverty of Spirit, of putting off our old Man, of renouncing our whole Selves, that we may see all Things in God; of watching and Prayer, and mortifying all our Inclinations, that our Hearts may be moved by a Motion from God, and our Wills and Inclinations be directed by the Light and Wisdom of Religion.

Religion has little or no hold of us, till we have these right Apprehensions of ourselves; it may serve for a little Decency of outward Behavior, but it is not the Religion of our Hearts, till we feel the weakness and disorder of our Nature, and embrace Piety and Devotion, as the Means of recovering us to a State of Perfection and Happiness in God.[74]

Here, as elsewhere, Law envisages devotion as including right thinking and right motive, as well as right action. He thereby enlists the full dedication and participation of man's total personality—intellect, temperament, and will. His views of devotional activity correspond strikingly to traditional concepts of that subject. As Helen McHugh notes of the devotional prose writers of an earlier period, "[they told] of the allness of the Creator, of the nothingness of the creature, of indifference and detachment, of the necessity for acquiring the preeminently Christian virtues of meekness and humility; they spoke of prayer, vocal and contemplative, of the preparation for prayer in good reading and in the word of the mind."[75] One cannot fail to see Law's kinship with those who fostered these ideals.

CHAPTER 3

Nondevotional Works: Controversy and Theology

I *The Bangorian Controversy*

L AW'S controversy with Bishop Hoadley, King's Chaplain and Latitudinarian Bishop of Bangor, was part of a larger controversy whether the king ruled by Divine Right and was, therefore, accountable to God alone, and whether hereditary right was indefeasible. Arguments for Divine Right of Kings were usually made from Scripture or from antiquity. Those who were loyal to William in 1688 argued for obedience to the powers that be, as St. Paul enjoined, pointing out that kingly power had changed hands violently in biblical times, that the teachings of the Church Fathers on the subject were inconclusive, and that later tradition failed to lend the doctrine strong support.

The controversy erupted in 1716 when a petition was circulated among Non-jurors recommending removal of certain defects from worship, especially respecting omissions from the Eucharist: the invocation and oblation, prayers for the faithful departed, and mixing water with wine. Lack of uniformity in worship was also deplored. Proposed amendments of the 1662 Prayer Book also stimulated a flurry of tracts between such men as Bishop Collier and Bishop Gandy. While Law seems to have sided with Collier, who favored certain amendments in the Prayer Book, he refused to be sidetracked from the larger issues that began to emerge.

A friend of Samuel Clarke and admirer of John Locke, Bishop Hoadley wrote *A Preservation Against the Principles and Practices of the Non-jurors Both in Church and State.* Hoadley supported the Whig cause, favoring the Protestant Succession, and had little appreciation for the Puritan position or the historical claims of the church. He therefore had little sympathy with the Thirty-Nine Articles or the Book of Common Prayer and was opposed to Protestant enthusiasm and High-Church sacerdotalism. Disregarding outward and visible ordinances, he contended for an "invisible" church—that a man's right to God's favor does not depend on any particular method, but relies rather on his real sincerity of conscience and actions. Although he believed Non-jurors should be prohibited by just procedure of civil law, he concluded that God made no rigid requirement to belong to a certain external communion. He argued that the "regularity of ordination and interrupted succession be mere trifles" and gave greater priority to private judgment than to tradition as a reliable guide in religion.[1] He also doubted that natural man had the power to grant absolution. Hoadley later attacked the authority of the church in a sermon published with the king's approval in 1717.

The Bishop's work caused a furor involving at least fifty divines. More than seventy-four pamphlets were written in July 1717 alone. Leslie Stephen comments, "The Controversy . . . is one of the most intricate tangles of fruitless logomacy in the language."[2]

Contrary to the Broad-Churchman's indifference to dogma, Law contended for the church as a living organism, with Christ as its head, with established ordinances, and with the Christian ministry as a continuation of the Apostolic Succession.

Law begins his first letter to the Bishop of Bangor (1717) by pointing out how the freethinkers, who openly favor dissolution of the Church of England, regard the Bishop rightfully as their ally in arguing that sincerity is all that matters in religion; such a belief is morally ambiguous. On the subject of church authority, Law argues that had Christ left no authorized succession of priests and sacraments or church there could be no Christian covenant, for the sacraments are the visible seal of covenant. While the Bishop had contended that Christ left no absolute authority behind, Law points out that the reasons Hoadley gives are really against any degree of authority and contrary to his own defense of a limited monarchy in English government. Sacraments, Law states, are real as a means of grace, though conditional and limited, as monarchy is real, though not absolute.

The first letter ends on a criticism of the Bishop's definition of prayer as "a calm and undisturbed address to God." Law contends that prayer is confession and petition, and perturbation of spirit in confession and fervor in petition are natural concomitants of prayer. Hence right passions are admissible. He redefines prayer as "an address to heaven, enlivened with such degrees and fervor and intenseness as our natural temper, influenced with a true sense of God, could beget in us."[3]

In his second letter (1717) Law answers the Bishop's arguments against "human benedictions, absolutions, human-excommunications" by pointing out how the tenor of the Scriptures sanctions God's deputizing men to act in His name and how the priestly office must assume a divine commission if it is to perform effectively in the world. And for Law "Episcopacy is the only instituted method of continuing the priesthood."[4] As a High Churchman, he defends the ecclesiastical tradition, appealing to the Scriptures, the Councils of the church, and Apostolic Succession. To Hoadley's assertion that fallible man could not grant absolution, Law contends that this argues against all the sacraments of the Christian faith, for no one can be infallibly sure that he qualifies to receive the sacraments or that he will even be saved.

In a postscript Law answers a main objection to his first letter: uninterrupted succession is not mentioned in the Scripture and, therefore, is not binding. He notes that neither are the priestly office and Sunday worship commanded in the Bible, but matters of apostolic practice ought to be decided from the tenor of the Scriptures and what seems right from the nature of things.

A third letter, published two years later (1719), replied to Hoadley's *Representation of the Committee*, which touched upon the nature of the church, excommunication, external communion, and the Reformation.

Hoadley had said that the church was invisible, but Law contends that the church must be visible to officiate in such practical matters as excommunication, administering communion, and assisting private judgment. To Hoadley's comment that the power of excommunication lies in all Christians, Law points out that the laws of the land by which we live argue for restriction of individual liberty; judicial power belongs to special persons. He points to the Scriptures that teach this doctrine.[5] Excommunication seeks to preserve the honor of God and the Church, to discipline offenders, and to act as a deterrent to license. It is as effective as human institutions can be. As for communion, he believes that external forms are naturally implied by Christianity itself. It is no more an indifferent matter than is schism.

To Hoadley's statement that if Church authority was required, the Reformation could not be justified, Law counters that with the Reformation the question was whether true religion was the Reformers' or the Papists'. Only the merits of Christ secure justification before God of either group.

Law gives a more ardent and fuller-bodied argument on the

nature of the sacrament in his reply to *A Plain Account of the Nature and End of the Sacrament of the Lord's Supper*, of which Hoadley was the alleged author. Hoadley held that the essential nature and meaning of the sacrament could be understood by us only in terms of the specific words of Christ on the subject. Law counters:

But if these Words are but a *Part* of the Christian Religion, if they are to be understood *according* to that *Religion* of which they are a Part, if the Articles of our Christian Salvation have any *Concern* in them, and we are to receive them as Christians in *such* a Sense as our *Christianity* requires of us; then it is undeniably certain, that this Author refers us to an *Absurdity*, and *Impossibility*, when he refers and confines us to the bare Words of the Institution, understood only according to the common Rules of speaking, in order to have a *Christian* Knowledge of the Holy Sacrament.[6]

Law contends that the Bishop's views are narrow—that the sacrament is to be observed as a "remembering" and "acknowledging" Christ as Lord as taught in the tenor of the Scriptures more than in the bare outlines of a few isolated passages. Christ is the principle of life and as such must be received by faith; eating His flesh and drinking His blood must, then, involve faith more than ritual. Unlike Hoadley's, Law's view of the sacraments coincided with that expressed in the Twenty-Fifth Article of the Church of England, "Sacraments ordained by Christ be not only badges or tokens of Christian men's profession, but rather they be certain sure witnesses, and effectual signs of grace, and God's good will towards us, by the which He doth work invisibly in us, and doth not only quicken, but also strengthen and confirm our faith in Him." That "God works invisibly in us" was at all times Law's firm belief. Increasingly during his late years he emphasized the constant feeding on Christ by faith as a means of grace more than the periodic receiving of the sacraments.

From the vantage point of the twentieth century one can see truth and bias on both sides in the controversy. Hoadley's distrust of authority and church tradition, his contention for an "invisible church," and his limited view of the sacrament have been shared by numerous adherents of the Christian church. Law, however, was quick to discern the liberalizing intellectual and religious tendencies in his opponent. Hoadley's emphasis upon sincerity as all that really matters in religion and his willingness to make religion personal rather than corporate represented for Law a Latitudinarian drift towards secularism.

The Latitudinarians had little interest in the historical claims of the church or in the sacramental teachings of the Thirty-Nine Articles or the Book of Common Prayer. They exalted the supremacy of reason in such matters, denounced enthusiasm, and urged a decorous life as the spiritual ideal. Hoadley's alleged attempt to be "reasonable" was viewed by Law as exalting reason unlawfully above tradition and Revelation.

It may be that on these points Law shrank too far from intellectual probing, even though theoretically he was committed to both tradition and rational examination. When he felt that reason had exceeded its rightful bounds, both his bias and conviction joined against further intellectual scrutiny. He became dogmatic, defensive, and perhaps less convincing than Hoadley when the latter declared the position of the Non-jurors to be untenable and doubted whether the Succession had been maintained. But Law perceived from afar the underlying dangers of Hoadley's overall position. He anticipated the dangers of higher criticism by irreverent minds who would raise serious intellectual questions about the authority of the Scriptures. His voice was to be heard by both Deists and Agnostics who accorded even greater status to the rational faculty.

That Law was hard-hitting is not doubted, but neither is his sense of fair play. He may have demolished Hoadley, but he never misrepresented the position of his opponent and had the rare ability to keep to the main point at issue. He refused to be sidetracked by such lesser matters as whether the Test Acts ought to be repealed or whether the Bishop's life was above reproach. His main point, as Overton suggests, was whether Hoadley's assertions did not "tend to impair the nature of the church in which he held office."[7]

Although Law's views in the Bangorian controversy paralleled those of the typical Anglican churchman, he was often much more extreme and intolerant than they. Adhering in the main to the Caroline method in theology, he claimed too much for the High Church position by identifying Anglicanism with it. The *via media* of Anglicanism has both Catholic and Reformed elements in it. Law's willingness to unchurch those who did not maintain a Catholic view of the sacrament and ministry was indeed more than the typical Anglican would consent to.

The issues discussed in the Bangorian controversy stimulated a widespread written response at the time; one leading churchman went so far as to aver that the letters to Hoadley "may fairly be put on a level with the *Lettres Provinciales* of Blaise Pascal."[8] Interest in them, however, has diminished to the point that Law's letters to the Bishop of Bangor are seldom read today. But through them one may become acquainted not only with his Anglican views, but also with his characteristic seriousness and his forceful and logical manner.

If the life and works of William Law are of "one piece," one may assume that even his controversial writing was for him no mere academic exercise. The intellectual assent for which he aimed was meant to be only the prelude to pious action. Dogma, therefore, while not his primary consideration, could not be ignored. His concern for right belief as preliminary to pious living continued in the devotional works where he emphasized repeatedly the importance of righteousness in both thought and deed.

II The Deistic Controversy: Reply to
Mandeville and Tindal

Law's *Remarks Upon a Late Book Entitled "The Fable of the Bees,"* published in 1723, attacked Bernard Mandeville's arguments against conventional morality. Mandeville, who had succeeded Hobbes as the apostle of irreligion, had rejected Shaftesbury's teaching that human nature is essentially good. He taught that the motive of human conduct is selfishness, either in obeying natural impulses or in subjecting them through desire to win praise or avoid censure. He had ridiculed the notion that honesty is the best policy and had rejected ascetic virtue and morality as exemplary goals for human conduct, contending that men, like the brutes, are governed by mere instinct and passion. "[*M*]*oral Virtues*," he said, "*are the political offspring which Flattery begot upon Pride.*" He tried to show that the welfare and prosperity of a community are dependent upon luxury and pride, which are vices in the individual. Smiths would be out of work if they gave up crime; we should dispute men's morals no more than their tastes. Charity is a passion rather than a virtue; custom rather than strict legality should be the guide to accepted practice.

Mandeville's point is that virtue is impracticable; it is to vice that we owe our benefits and why not recognize it, if we would be honest? Mandeville admitted to a high concept of virtue, but he said that men do not behave that way. And since good things happen in the world without self-control and rational behavior, why not accept the human predicament? Man should be viewed for what he is rather than for what he should be. F. B. Kaye points out that Mandeville's reasoning is based on two divergent concepts of virtue common in the eighteenth century, one ascetic, in which virtue was to be achieved through self-conquest and divine grace, and the other rationalistic, in which virtue was accepted as being in accord with the dictates of reason. By accepting both of these conflicting definitions, Mandeville demonstrated the social impracticality of the usual ideals of conduct.[9]

Law was diametrically opposed to Mandeville's cynical views of human nature and moral idealism. Virtue originated, he contended, not in acts of sagacity or cunning of philosophers, but in God's creation of man in His own image. Moral virtue is founded upon the "immutable relations of things"—upon the perfection and attributes of God rather than in the pride of man. God had also declared the excellence of man's potential and had filled man's mind with high and noble desires. Law extolled the faculty of reason bestowed by God, as that which governs the actions and gives peace to the mind of man.

Law also opposed Mandeville's contention that man in a state of nature is savage and brutal without any notions of morality or ideas of religion. As proof of a time when all men were virtuous, Law cited Noah's knowledge of virtue and morality as he and his family emerged from the ark to start a new race. Mandeville, Law contended, was forming an opinion of human nature upon the tempers and practice of Christians and yet on the other hand pretending to treat man in such a state of nature as he never saw in his life.

Although *The Fable of the Bees* is not always associated with the Deist controversy, a study by A. Owen Aldridge quotes several sections of Mandeville's work to show that the latter contributed to the deistic attempt to exalt natural religion and to ridicule all forms of orthodox faith.[10] In addition to believing in the transcendence of God, the Deist contended that one could see and revere God as the great architect of the universe without resorting to miracles or theological doctrines of the Incarnation and Trinity. He believed that after death virtue would be rewarded and sin punished.

That Law was distrustful of the Deist's plan to place religion upon a completely rational basis is evident; somewhat paradoxically, however, he distinguishes himself from most of his predecessors in devotional literature who make authority the sole basis for all religious requirements by attempting continually to demonstrate the reasonableness of Christianity.

At the points where religion makes its greatest demands, Law anticipates the counter arguments which may be raised, showing how the demands are not arbitrary, but rather are founded upon right reason. The following passage is typical:

> Every Duty or virtue of the Christian life is founded in Truth and Reason, and is required because of its Fitness to be done, and not because God has Power to command what he pleases. . . .

. . . When our Lives are conformable to the highest Reason, then may we
believe that so far as they are such, so far are they in the Favor of God, who is
the highest Reason.[11]

Law's views of Scripture and reason are not unlike those of such
seventeenth-century divines as Donne and Andrewes. For them, the
Scriptures were indisputably holy, inspired, and authoritative. With
their conviction of the importance of the moral sense, they came to
believe that what is most true is that which can be clearly and
distinctly conceived. That which is inscribed upon the minds of all
men and which is approved by the general sense is consonant with
nature and reason. Still adhering to belief in the Scripture's authority,
they viewed reason as being in agreement with Revelation.

With the rise of Deism and natural religion in the eighteenth
century and the renewed efforts of the rationalists, the position of the
Scriptures as the only valid authority in religion came into question.
Men did not regard the Scriptures as "false," but inclined more and
more to "natural religion" as a sufficient revelation of God. Deity
could be seen as clearly in the starry heavens above and the moral law
within. Law's views of Revelation and reason, on the other hand,
were much more like those of the theologians of the seventeenth
century.

One might suppose that Law would have found much to admire in
the Cambridge Platonists who made reason "the candle of the Lord."
There is, however, some disagreement on this point. Bishop Ralph
Inge says that Law was well acquainted only with Henry More, and
while he admired the latter's character, he considered him an enemy
of the "innerlight" and his books a "jumble of rant."[12] Stephen
Hobhouse, however, disagrees with Inge, pointing to the seven books
of the Cambridge Platonists which are still in the Law library and
contending that there was considerable affinity between Law and his
predecessors, Henry More, John Smith, Cudworth, Whichcote, and
Norris.[13] It is very probable that Law was familiar with the teaching
of the Cambridge Platonists and reproduced some of their ideas in his
works without always acknowledging them.

For Law, God is the embodiment of infinite reason; therefore the
ways of God conform to the dictates of right reason. Properly
exercised, man's rational faculties may perceive God's ways and
dictate right action, although of course man's rational powers have
been impaired by his innate sinfulness. Through such a firm belief in
reason's correspondence to the ways of God, without minimizing
scriptural authority, Law manifests his willingness to go partway

with the eighteenth-century's stress upon the use of reason as a dependable guide to religion. At the same time he recognizes the limitations of reason's power.

In general, Deism is concerned with the relation of reason and Revelation, the truth and authority of Scripture, the evidential value of miracles, and the relative importance of natural and revealed religion. At first, as one historical study by Samuel Hefelbower states, "the old statements concerning the relation of reason and Revelation, which had come down from Thomas Aquinas, were accepted by all deistic thinkers. They taught that Revelation could give that which was above reason, but nothing contrary to reason."[14] The father of English Deism, Herbert of Cherbury, concurred in this, but later deists Charles Blount and John Toland emphasized that "there is nothing in the gospel contrary to reason nor above it." This became the new thrust of the deistic arguments in the century. The fact of Revelation was not always denied, but the controversy turned upon evidence for it and whether it added to the truths of natural religion.

Sometimes theologians like Samuel Clarke rehearsed the evidences for Revelation found in the world about them. John Locke, who based all knowledge upon sensation and reflection, accepted Revelation only because he thought there was sufficient external evidence to support it. Berkeley, Butler, and Hume were also concerned with the foundations of natural religion. Berkeley implied a belief in God and spiritual interpretation of all the world through a survey of experience. Hume, by pursuing the principles of Locke and Berkeley to their logical conclusions, showed the need for a deeper basis for religious faith than the arguments being used.

The triumph of natural religion resulted in reducing Revelation as a mere accompaniment of faith, lessened the stress on asceticism and original sin, and equated religious life with the practice of virtue. As religious historian Mark Pattison points out, the appeal to reason was "a first effort of English theology to find a new basis for doctrine to replace the foundations which had failed it."[15]

Law did not differ with Mandeville and the Deists in all their pronouncements about man's depravity and God's transcendence. However, he opposed violently their depreciation of scriptural Revelation and their apotheosis of reason. To him, their views were at best remote and could lead only to skepticism. At least one writer described Law's *Remarks Upon . . . The Fable of the Bees* as "one of the most remarkable philosophical essays" he had ever seen in English: "I have never seen in our language the elementary ground of a rational, ideal philosophy as opposed to empiricism stated in nearly the same calmness, simplicity, and force."[16] Leslie Stephen called it "the ablest of the attacks on Mandeville."[17]

The whole discussion of natural religion was an integral part of the Deist controversy. Deism as a movement was linked with the Hobbes-Locke controversy preceding it and is not, therefore, to be thought of as a separate radical movement appearing without roots in the past. The moralists of the early eighteenth century, like the rationalists of the late seventeenth century, were stimulated by opposition to the view of Hobbes. All of them were concerned with benevolence and its relation to self-love, as well as to virtue.

In 1731 Law wrote his principal defense against natural religion in *The Case of Reason or Natural Religion Fairly and Fully Stated*. Answering a book entitled *Christianity as Old as Creation* (1730), allegedly written by Matthew Tindal, Law refutes the proposition that "no religion can come from God which teaches anything more than that which is fully manifest to all mankind by the *mere light* of nature." He denies that human reason, or natural light, apart from divine revelation, is a sufficient guide in religion, that anything admitted as a matter of religion not manifest from reason is superstition, and that human reason is the only means of knowing all that God requires of us. Bishop Butler in his *Analogy of Religion* pursued the same argument. Both Law and Butler agreed that man needed divine assistance to atone for or repent of his sins, Butler arguing from the analogy of man's general inability to comprehend anything and Law arguing from the limitations imposed upon man by the fall.

Law argued that human reason cannot be trusted as an arbiter between God and man of all that ought or ought not to comprise holy religion. To say that reason is the "universal agent" in natural man is no more unprejudiced than to say that "a sinner is *sinless*, or a man is an *angel*." Man may as well be governed by his passions as rely upon unenlightened reason. He concludes, "To resign ourselves up to our reason, to tell us what ought, or ought not to be a matter of religion, is only resigning ourselves up to our tempers, to take what we *like*, and refuse what we *dislike* in religion."[18]

As church historian John Overton states, Tindal argued for the "eternal and immutable fitness of things" more than the will of God as the basis for morality. Law does not think that man is able to figure out the "fitness of things" and prefers to trust in the more certain way of Revelation. If fitness of actions is founded on the nature of things, then fitness must be what God considers it, and God is incomprehensible. Locke's treatise, *The Reasonableness of Christianity*, reinforced the Deists' arguments that were being used. Law cited the shortcomings of reason as illustrating the paradox of man's will, where man receives everything from God and yet is free to exercise choice. The divine will might be natural to us if we could understand it. Revelation and miracles are necessary, for they divulge and achieve what mere reason could never do.

One rightly expects in the eighteenth century a sharp impact by reason upon religious thought. To prove that the church teachings were true because they were reasonable was the special work of such Latitudinarians as Burnet, Stillingfleet, and Tenison:

To assert the reasonableness of the Church, to prove that religion is agreeable to common sense, and that the practice of virtue brings its own reward even in this life, to deprecate excitement, to denounce the dangers of fanaticism, to disprove the reality of special spiritual illumination, to insist upon the excellence of moderation—such were the lessons which the eighteenth-century Latitudinarian had to teach.[19]

Law's occasional limitation of the power of human reason at first may seem to set him apart from the intellectual context of an age that extolled rationalistic ideals. Law, however, rather than denying reason's power or validity, was simply setting limitations on it. He never repudiates reason as long as man uses it moderately and subverts it to divine grace. "His sensitiveness to logic was as marked as his sensitiveness to conscience."[20] In fact, the devotional works themselves are filled with exhortations to live piously simply because it is the reasonable thing to do; right practice usually corresponds to right reason. But true reason for Law means thinking God's thoughts with Him, which is virtually impossible in the state of sin into which man has fallen. By reason, Tindal meant "human reason" acting by itself, while to Law it meant man's sharing in the infinite reason of God, recognizing the limitations on the mind brought about by depravity. In the main, Law prefers scriptural authority as a more reliable standard and basis for pious conduct than reason.

Law's position is much like that of the conservative-minded High Churchman, with an added mystical bent. His deep feeling about the mysteries of religion contrasts sharply with Tindal's more academic approach. Law, like Joseph Butler, sees nature as obscure and perplexing; Butler, however, adheres more strictly to ratiocination, preferring to speak more cautiously of the "probable" truth of the Christian system on the "assumption" that there is a God.

Law points out the difficulties that accompany the arguments of the Deists. One notes clearly his willingness to use what he calls "vision" and "imagination" to supplement reason in philosophical and theological questions. His argument is cogent, and his painstaking and fervent manner win for him the plaudits of such historians and thinkers as Leslie Stephen and Arthur Hopkinson, the first lauding Law's vigorous logic and the second commending his lofty spiritual goals.[21] As Arthur Hopkinson points out, Law's aim was the conversion of his readers. The step to writing of a strictly devotional sort was, consequently, a short one, for right belief is always a prime prerequisite to righteous living.

III   Minor Controversies: Trapp and Warburton

Two other brief controversial writings were *An Earnest and Serious Answer to Dr. Trapp's Discourse of the Folly, Sin, and Danger of Being Righteous Overmuch* (1740)[22] and *A Short but Sufficient Confutation of the Reverend Dr. Warburton's Projected Defence of Christianity* (1737). Joseph Trapp, a Tory, a High Churchman, and first Professor of Poetry at Oxford, reflected the typical Anglican's contempt for religious enthusiasm. His *Discourse* built its argument rather precariously upon Ecclesiastes 7:16, "Be not righteous overmuch." He upheld the Aristotelian doctrine of the mean: "When virtue rises beyond its due bounds, it loses its nature and degenerates into vice; and since it loses its nature it ought to lose its name." Trapp earlier had expressed his opinion that *Christian Perfection* and *A Serious Call* would have only a harmful effect upon the public mind because of their encouragement of religious enthusiasm and he pointed to the emotionalism of the Methodists as illustration of the religious extremes to which men might go.

Of course, Trapp's sentiments represented the very spirit that Law consecrated his whole life to thwart. Law assailed ecclesiastical complacency by emphasizing the fallen state of man and his need for purification and expressed a deep concern over the eighteenth century's indifference to perfection and scorn for religious enthusiasm. Law rehearsed the implications of man's fall from a state of paradise, along with necessary steps for reinstatement in God's favor. Earth is the place for man to put off his "filthy and defiled garments." Hence he should use every means to recover his Adamic nature.

In his reply Law emphasized again the need for self-denial and self-discipline among clergymen. Trapp had previously derided *Christian Perfection* for its complete lack of interest in material things. In restrained, but solemn, language Law defended *Christian Perfection* with frequent allusion to the life of Christ and such New Testament teachings as "Be ye therefore perfect even as your Father which is in heaven is perfect." The following passage is typical of his Puritan emphasis upon knowing the divine life in the present world:

Therefore all that we see and know of the Kingdom of God *now*, must be by that *same Light* by which we shall see and know the Kingdom of God hereafter. God is an *all-speaking, all-working*, all-illuminating Essence, possessing the Depth, and bringing forth the Life of every Creature according to its Nature. Our Life is out of this Divine Essence, and is itself a creaturely Similitude of it; and when we turn from all Impediments, this Divine Essence becomes as *certainly* the true Light of our Minds *here*, as it will be Hereafter.[23]

Actually, Law's doctrine continues in the true tradition of the High Churchman, with a Puritan estimate of the Christian's real relation with the world.

Law's argument with Bishop Warburton was over the latter's belief that the doctrine of immortality of the soul was entirely unknown among the earlier dispensations—until Christ and the New Testament writers propounded it to the Christian world. Warburton said that previously the designs of God concerning future existence were hidden. Law asserted to the contrary:

. . . There is not in all the New Testament, one single Text, which either in the Letter, or the Spirit proves, or has the least Tendency, or Design to prove, that the *Immortality* of the Soul, or its *perpetual Duration* after the Death of the Body, was not an *universal, commonly* received Opinion in, and through every Age of the World from *Adam* to Christ. . . . This Doctrine, or Belief of a future State, was not *designedly secreted*, or *industriously hidden* from the Eyes of the People of God by *Moses*, neither by the Types and Figures of the Law, nor by any other Part of his writings.[24]

Law attempted to show that the Jews must have had a good prospect of life and immortality, even in the dispensations of ceremonial religion and rule of moral law. He argued for the unity of the patriarchal and Christian religion. Only one spirit was working in man from the beginning of the world. The comfort and hope of immortality were available to St. Paul and Moses alike. More specifically, Law attacked the texts used by Warburton to support his views as "not touching in the least degree the one great point in question" and certainly not proving that the doctrine of the soul's

immortality was unknown through every age prior to Christ's coming
in the flesh.

Warburton built his case primarily upon St. Paul's statement,
"[God] hath saved us, and called us with a holy calling not according
to our works, but according to His purpose and grace, which was
given us in Christ Jesus before the world began, but is now made
manifest by the appearing of our Savior Jesus Christ, who hath
abolished death, and hath brought life and immortality to light
through the gospel."[25] He saw two time periods in St. Paul's account,
one when the secret counsels of God were formed, and the other when
the counsels were published to man. Warburton contended that
during the intervening period knowledge was kept secret, as he
believed the text implies.

It was Law's contention that Warburton's text did not refer to the
doctrine of the soul's future existence at all; rather, "life and
immortality" mean the progress out of the eternal death of sin and
misery into a participation in a heavenly life. The "mystery" opened
in the gospel means the existence and knowledge of the process to
change and purify the whole sinful state and nature of fallen man and
to bring again the eternal word and spirit of God into the natural life
of the soul. Nothing more or less is meant by "life and immortality"
than is meant by the new birth. Law argued also that free will or the
"will-spirit" in man partakes of the divine nature and, therefore, has
an eternal, indissoluble quality in it.

Warburton's basic assumption was repugnant to Law: that man,
who was born in an ignorant and brutal state, needed to be educated
gradually to understand the mysteries of God. Law argued that just as
God is immortal and man is made in the image of God, so the
knowledge of the immortality of the divine nature is essential to and
inseparable from the mind of man in any age. The knowledge of a
future state was, therefore, the foundation of even the patriarchal
religion. The arguments on both sides in this controversy were
spirited and temporarily engrossing, but the issues were drawn along
familiar lines and the outcome was without great consequence.

IV   *Works of Theology*

During his earlier years Law was seldom concerned with doctrinal
formularies, but when the public began to resist his mystical
emphasis, he turned in his later works to more elaborate explanations of his beliefs; his debt to new influences may then be readily
discerned.

Law's first encounter with mystical thought really began during his days at the university, where, in addition to reading the classics and the Church Fathers, he became familiar with the teachings of Nicholas Malebranche. The shelves of Law's library at King's Cliffe later contained numerous mystical works, including those of Dionysius the Areopagite, Meister Eckhart, Johannes Tauler, Henry Suso, and Jan Van Ruysbroeck. Law also valued highly the *Theologia Germanica*, which contained a kind of summary of mystical theology, but he owed his greatest debt to Jacob Boehme, whom he began to read about 1735. Of the five quartos that make up Boehme's works, Law draws most consistently from *Aurora, The Principles of the Divine Essence, De Signatura Rerum, The Threefold Life of Man*, and *Mysterium Magnum*. Law tells us that he learned High Dutch in order to master the *Aurora* in the original. The German's mystically conceived theological system provided a detailed cosmology and answers to such questions as, where did sin arise and how does God manifest Himself to this visible world? Law immersed himself in Boehme's teachings, for he found in them a satisfying myth for some of life's inscrutable mysteries.

The Grounds and Reasons of Christian Regeneration (1739) and *An Appeal to All Who Doubt the Truths of the Gospel* (1740) present the heart of Law's later theology. The former work provided another counter statement to Deism. The starting premise is that man is a trinity—body, soul, and spirit—made in the image of God. Law then describes for believers and unbelievers alike the spiritual condition of original man, how he fell from a pristine state, what the fall involved, and how a spiritual restoration became possible. He says, "Man was created by God *after his own Image*, and in his own Likeness, a living mirror of the *Divine Nature*: where Father, Son, and Holy Ghost each brought forth [His] *own Nature* in a *creaturely Manner*."[26] Inasmuch as man was made a separate personality, he could choose permanently to withdraw from the spiritual into the perishable world. This he did by turning his eyes from the heavenly light and viewing his own nakedness. With this, "discord and contrariety" broke forth, the life of God in the soul was extinguished, and man became identified with the earth element, fire, which Law calls the "hell" in his own nature.

According to Boehme, whom Law is following here, man must first know how sin arose before he can seek the remedy for it. This involved knowing how God first manifested Himself and how Contrary Will and all the "seven forms of nature" arose. Two principles are eternal: the dark world of anger (wrath) and light (characterized by love); the second principle, the present world, is a temporal place where good and evil strive for mastery. Man inclines his imagination to one of the eternal principles and eventually becomes identified with it permanently.

The seven forms of nature arose in the following order, according to Boehme: (1) *Harshness*, or self-centeredness, is present; (2) *Attraction*, or a principle of dissatisfaction or unrest moves one to constant activity; (3) *Bitterness*, or tension, arises from the conflict of the first two; (4) out of tension arises *Fire*, as well as self-consciousness, and the sense of personal choice; (5) *Light*, or the divine spark, enables one to see things as they are. This light changes fire to a pleasant warmth and helps one to see things aright; (6) *Sound* then follows, or ways a being has for expressing himself—by cries, tastes, scents, and the like; (7) *Figure* is the putting on of a body in which the various forms find expression.[27]

The key point in this evolutionary plan is the fourth form where the will either asserts itself selfishly, raising fire to a consuming flame, or unselfishly to produce illuminating warm love. The first three forms of nature are an essential part of every being, but they are known only to God. When man undertakes to bring these forms out of "hiddenness," and ascribes them to himself, sin arises. When he allows light to prevail, his imagination is illuminated and he understands reality. The sin he brings upon himself occurs only when he exercises a false imagination.

The four elements of the fiery soul, or fallen nature, are selfishness, envy, pride, and wrath, or anger. These discordant elements in man must be dealt with in a special way: selfishness, by resignation to God; envy, by universal love; pride, by humility; and wrath, by meekness. However, no single act can accomplish all the necessary changes; man's nature must be altered completely. The "seed of the new birth," or desire to turn to God, is latent in all men. The rebirth of God in the soul may be achieved in an instant, but all that was lost in Adam can be restored but gradually through self-denial and conformity to God's will.

Again, according to Boehme and Law, Adam did not lose the entire ability to know good; there remained in him a latent potential or divine "spark." But this could only be reached through a rebirth of spiritual life. Man must have the life of Christ in his false imagination. He avails himself of Christ's atonement, entering by faith into Christ's life and death by refusing the temptations of the world, the flesh, and the devil (i.e., the lust of the flesh, the lust of the eyes, and the pride of life). Thus, he regains what Adam lost by realigning his will with God's will.

Similar to William Blake's later position that "without contraries is no progression," the central postulate of Boehme's philosophy affirms that all manifestation necessitates opposition. He explains body, soul, and spirit as thesis, antithesis, and synthesis—the same formula he uses to explain good, evil, and free will. Good can be known only through evil, just as light is evident only when reflected by a dark body. God becomes manifest when out of His own "hidden" nature He divides the will into "yes" and "no" and lets them struggle for supremacy. Finally, the cosmic process will exhibit victory of Good over Evil, or Love over Hatred.

In *An Appeal to All That Doubt the Truths of the Gospel* (1740), Law furnishes no new doctrine. Writing under the new mystical influences, he inclines to more speculation about the nature of things, ostensibly to counter the "Deists, Arians, Socinians, and nominal Christians," whom he mentions in his full title. He begins with the Genesis account of creation. God made man a "living soul" in the image of God, who was light, life, and spirit. Law asserts that inasmuch as "thinking" and "willing" are eternal with God, when man became a separate entity in God's likeness, he still possessed these qualities. The delight in and desire of eternal existence are still strong in man. Since the soul is made of eternal substance, it will naturally seek God as that which is most like itself. The account of the fall of the soul, then, parallels very closely that in *Grounds and Reasons of Christian Regeneration.*

Chapter two relates how all matter is nothing but the materiality of heaven altered—"separated, divided, compacted, made visible." As such it is dead, gross, and dark because it is broken off from its source. The darkness can be brought to life by the power, fire, and light, as is illustrated in nature by the light and heat of the sun. Similarly, intelligent creatures formed out of the harmonious union of fire, light, and spirit for the enjoyment of the Divine Kingdom, broke off from their source in the beings of Lucifer and Adam. Removed from their original light, they knew only the dark, wrathful fire, which had to be quenched so the soul could once more have the Triune Life of God in it. The desire was still present in man to know life or death. Fire, or desire, exists in all creatures. Desire for the earthly is called "hell," and for the eternal, "heaven."

The final chapter points up the necessity of the Incarnation. The life, suffering, death, resurrection, and ascension of the Son of God were necessary to bring about His birth in man, for Adam could not raise himself to the state from which he had fallen. Only the One who possessed infinite love and perfect light could bring light and love again to the soul. This, says Law, is the basis of the shedding of blood for sin. The sacrifice of a life to regain life made possible man's restoration to his original image.

Blood has a life-giving quality about it. It is that blood which is received in the Holy Sacrament. We now get a heavenly, immortal flesh and blood from heaven—the same kind that was in Adam originally. The view of the sacrament here expressed becomes much more mystical than that held heretofore.

Another theological work appearing in 1760 was entitled *Of Justification by Faith and Works: A Dialogue between a Methodist and a Churchman.* Quite brief, and evidently directed toward the Calvinistic branch of theology, it discusses St. Paul's text in Galatians 2:16, "We have believed in Jesus Christ that we might be justified by the faith of Christ and not by the works of the law." Law objects to salvation partly by works and partly by faith as "false and groundless" and asserts that the imputed righteousness of Christ is of no consequence unless the believer receives newness of life:

Trust in anything else, seek to anything else, but the Process of Christ, and this power of the Holy Ghost, and then all your leaning upon the Gospel will be no better than leaning upon a broken reed.[28]

Throughout the argument Law reiterates many of the ideas advanced in his earlier works. His principal objection is to the doctrine that men can ascribe efficacy to good works apart from faith. As elsewhere, Law insists that salvation means, above all else, new life through redemptive faith.

The main outlines of Law's theology have not changed significantly in *An Appeal....* Even as he celebrates the extra-biblical details of Boehme's theological system, evil is still his main burden. The work is similar to the devotional writings in its plea to contemplate righteousness. Some have admired its refined spirituality: C. S. Lewis said of it, "I like it as well as any religious work I have ever read. The prose of the *Serious Call* has been melted away and the book is saturated with delight and the sense of wonder. . . ."[29] Stephen Hobhouse calls it "the best . . . statement of mystical theology and cosmology."[30]

V   *Theological Alterations*

Although the foregoing works have been classified as "theological" or "controversial" because the devotional motif is not dominant, doctrine and religious argument tell us a great deal about Law's basic beliefs which have elicited the most critical comment. Even here one notes everywhere what Hopkinson calls his "Augustinian sense of reverence," his zeal for righteousness, and his utter sincerity in obeying what he believed to be the voice of the Spirit.[31]

A quick comparison of Law's "early" and "late" works reveals some shifts in thought and emphasis. Those who have disapproved of his new mystical tendencies or recurring failures to allude to Scripture as much as formerly have occasionally branded him "heterodox." Some of the grounds for these doctrinal criticisms are the following: (1) Increased stress upon the indwelling presence of Christ, or imparted righteousness, with diminished recognition of the Calvinistic doctrine of imputed righteousness; (2) interest in heaven and hell as states of the soul rather than separate abodes; (3) belief in the "real presence" of Christ in the Eucharist; (4) intimation that the soul is not created *ex nihilo*, but is a spark of the Divine Being; (5) insisting not only upon the death of Christ, but the whole process of salvation as necessary to restoration of new life in man: incarnation, passion, death, resurrection, ascension; (6) belief in a God of love that cannot be harmonized with a God of wrath, which is tantamount to Universalism.

When one reviews the bases for concern over Law's alleged heterodoxy (that is, for views outside the mainstream of historical Reformed-Catholic tradition), he is struck with two things: first, if Law does deviate from orthodoxy, it is purely inadvertent, for he always uses the Scriptures as his starting point and authority. In both the early and late works he is at heart the Anglican priest. Whatever strange sounds he may emit are but new interpretations or elaborations of truths he has always affirmed. A second point is that what is sometimes thought to be a change in doctrine is merely a shift in emphasis.

Most of Law's alterations have been exaggerated or ignored as following some precedent in the Established Church. For instance, he is not the first to emphasize imparted righteousness (as opposed to imputed righteousness), or hell as a state of the alienated soul (as opposed to a specific place). Similarly, his belief in angelic perfection for man, affirmed as early as *Christian Perfection* and reiterated ardently throughout the mystical works, represented a lofty and refined concept of human restoration, but can hardly be viewed as having no historical precedent.

On this last point, however, Law does amplify the idea of man's loss of original, angelic perfection and his repairing the fall of angels from heaven by "a race of angelic men born on earth." In the mystical works he explains how the Trinity was reproduced in man: Adam possessed originally in himself the virgin perfection of life; Eve, the female part of him, was still joined to his nature. The soul of Adam purports to be a mirror of the Holy Trinity; it is the breath of life from the mouth of God. Since the makeup of God is tripartite, and man was made in His image, then the soul of man must be in three parts. According to this explanation, man's personality is made up of fire, light, and air. Sin deprives him of the light of Christ but not the fire substance of the Creator, thus disintegrating the trinity in man. Law says that he does not take this from any known source, but it could have come from Boehme or Ruysbroeck. Even the older theologians, Augustine, St. Bernard, and Bonaventura, interpreted Genesis 1:26 as signifying a trinity in man, although they were not always agreed upon the exact nature of that trinity.

This view, Law believes, is tenable, not only because the Scripture affords grounds for it, but because all he knows about the makeup of the elements of the world and spirit, and the mutual attraction which likes have for their opposites, support it:

> . . . everything in Nature, Fire, and Light, and Air; everything that we know of Angels, of Devils, and of the animal Life of this World; are all in the plainest and strongest manner . . . made so many Proofs of the threefold Life of the triune God in the Soul . . . the Fire, and Light, and Air of this world, must have their Birth in your own creaturely Being, or you cannot possibly live in, or have a Life from *outward Nature.* And therefore no Omnipotence can make you a Partaker of the beatific Life, or Presence of the Holy Trinity, unless that Life stands in the same triune State within you, as it does without you.[32]

This theory of the world and man is discussed at length in *An Appeal to All Who Doubt . . .* and *Christian Regeneration.* Theologians have generally agreed that man is created in the image of God, but, as Hobhouse explains, not all of them have agreed on just how the Trinity was reproduced in man, although Augustine, Bonaventura, and others theorize about it.

Perhaps the most consistent criticism of Law's later theology is leveled at his alleged Universalism, or the belief that eventually all men will be saved, with or without their cooperation. The charge is made on very flimsy evidence deduced largely from the implications of several passages or from his emphasis upon a God of love rather than a God of justice. From the very outset it is hard to see how his strong emphasis upon the priority of will fits into a Universalist scheme where good wins automatically over evil.

Holding to the axiom that God is love, Law naturally was led to ask how evil could arise in a universe made and governed by a God of love. He began his inquiry with the fall of the angels, for they were the first free moral agents. Everything as made by God was perfect and good, he concluded. But the noblest of gifts, free will, which was conferred on man, gave him a kind of divine omnipotence, and enabled him to choose a new state. Just as the angels fell by separating themselves from the divine light unto the dark and wrathful fire of hell, so man was capable of falling away from his divine nature.

The command of God had been that man must not disobey or he would fall into misery. This was not arbitrarily or vindictively imposed, but was the decree of an all-loving God who permitted man to have what he willfully chose.

Law spoke of the seed of the divine life being implanted in Adam after the fall, asserting that salvation in the beginning was hidden under the veil of the law until it was made manifest in the second Adam. This restoration by the second Adam was complete and efficacious for all men. Hence, the universality of the atonement was realized. But always Law makes plain that this salvation must be embraced; it is *contingent* upon *choice*. If man persisted in willful disobedience, he continued indefinitely in a state of separation from God. The following selection gives Law's representative view:

. . . But if you die without this Birth of Eternal Light and Spirit of God, then your Soul stands in the *same Distance* from, and *Contrariety* to the Kingdom of Heaven, as Hell does: If you die in this unregenerate State, it signifies nothing *how* you have lived, or *what* Religion you have owned, all is left undone that was to have saved you.[33]

It is true that Law contemplates the possibility of the complete restoration of men and angels at some future time. A few remarks in his letters and late works hint that the idea of complete redemption made this a possibility. Thomas Langcake said that in conversation with Law a few days before the latter's death Law indicated he was about to believe that the whole human race and even the fallen angels would be delivered out of misery by the Judgment Day.[34] However, the tenor of Law's teachings falls short of declaring man's universal redemption—*unless he wills it.* The notion that some were predestined to be saved and others to be damned was also repugnant to him for the same reason that man's volitional power was ignored.

Law, however, did emphasize that God is love and that His dealings with the universe must be consistent with it. God's creation of the world as a place to restore communion and man's creation to take the place vacated by the fallen angels testify to His love. As the fall was primarily a loss of divine life, so redemption must be renewal of that life *via* the new birth. And if the first Adam died to the Kingdom of Heaven through exercise of choice, so the second Adam successfully brought the Kingdom back within the reach of all through successful resistance to temptation.

Believing that God was essentially love, Law could not reconcile wrath with God's nature. The traditional teaching that the death of Christ is necessary as an "atonement" or "satisfaction" for the wrath of an offended Deity was offensive to him. Still intent upon leading his reader to the devotional heights of godlikeness through repossession of the pristine purity which he once lost, Law bypasses the more familiar biblical explanation of the atonement. Taking his cue from Boehme, he asserts that the spirit of love "gives," "forgives," "forbears," without thought of time or place or persons. He shows that the scriptural accounts of John 3:16, Colossians 1:12, 13, and Ephesians 1:3, instead of teaching that the love and compassion of God toward fallen men are purchased through the atonement, really portray the antecedent and continuing love of God for man. Law can find little to support the claim that offended Deity required the death of His Son as a satisfaction of offended justice.

Inasmuch as both Law and Boehme agreed that knowledge of God's ways is necessary to spiritual recovery and devotional admonition, it is only natural that Law would make his own version of the atonement and the new birth, which derive from such biblical sources as John 1:13 and 1 John 3:9.[35] Historically, two main doctrines of the atonement have prevailed: (1) Christ is a substitute for us; He was sacrificed in our stead as the "propitiation" for sin to satisfy the demands of offended justice; (2) Christ's death was meant to be an identification with suffering mankind in which He imparts his own nature and life to man. The first view stresses the legalistic necessity of an atoning sacrifice; the second centers more upon the resumption of new life in God. Law's preference was for the second; in fact, he was often critical of any thought of Christ's death serving any legalistic purpose. In this he was at variance with one mainstream of church tradition.

Such men as Wesley, Augustine, and Luther believed that the atonement meant primarily the removal of past guilt and a satisfaction of offended justice. Law's position was not without precedent, however, as Hobhouse reminds us; Irenaeus (ca. 180 A.D.) agreed with Law.[36] The Church of England, although it generally followed Calvin's and Luther's position, was quite diversified in its views of the atonement; neither were the medieval churchmen always as consistent in their views as the reformers. It may also be added that Law kept in mind the broader etymological connotations of at-onement, the making of God and man one, which represented a universal aspect of the meaning of that term. In any case, Law's variations from standard belief represented more a positive emphasis upon union with the divine life than a denial of traditional concepts.

Also radiating from Law's belief in a God of love was his analysis of man's unregenerate state. Believing that hell is a state of the soul more than a separate place where foul spirits go, he described at length the desolate inner condition. Deep inside man existed a dark, fallen spirit disunited from peace and joy. This state of separation from God was the essence of hell and punishment. Belief in hell as a state more than a place where wicked spirits finally go, while not dominant in church history, is not without historical precedent.

One readily understands Law's directives in the late devotional works for the worshiper to rid himself of his wrathful, impure, and unjust temper. Even those who were dissatisfied with Law's failure to locate hell in a separate place were bound to agree with his description of the inner state and the need for every exhortation and spiritual aid that he espoused. Law's continued insistence upon grace as the antidote for man's unregenerate condition can be realized only by appropriation of faith. Salvation is not automatic nor extended to all apart from willful cooperation. Those who make much of Law's Universalism usually supply what they think he is implying rather than interpreting a system of settled belief. His concern was to portray the deadliness of man's state rather than to deny a literal existence of hell.

Law's alleged minimizing of the importance of church attendance and his accent upon the validity of personal inspiration have also been overdrawn by his critics. The first point had been deduced from a comment in *A Serious Call*, "there is not one command in all the Gospel for *Public Worship*. . . ." This offended some staunch church-men, but Law, in spite of his Non-juror status, was not anti-church, as his own faithful attendance at public worship indicates; also, as he explained to John Wesley and others, his remark meant to make clear that attending church was secondary to a living faith.

Law's views of personal inspiration, although very much like those of such introspective devotionalists as Madame Guyon and St. Augustine, were not shared by most other members of the Anglican Church. Law evidently was not on the side of those who held to a special kind of inspiration for the books in the Hebrew Canon:

What a Mistake is it, therefore, to confine Inspiration to *particular* Times and Occasions, to Prophets and Apostles, and extraordinary Messengers of God, and to call it *Enthusiasm*, when the common Christian looks, and trusts to be *continually led* and inspired by the Spirit of God![37]

To him, the work of the Spirit in the heart of the believer was as supernatural as any more publicized revelation. He was not diverted from this view by contemporary churchmen who scorned the "inner-light" doctrine of the Quakers and the enthusiasm of the Methodists. Law was faithful to the inner vision and proclaimed it as the rightful heritage of every believer. If St. Paul's claim to immortality rests on his claim before King Agrippa, "I was not disobedient to the heavenly vision," William Law also deserves a niche in the hall of the immortals, for few men were more faithful than he to the heavenly vision. No teacher, or preacher, was ever more intent than he to lift the sights of his fellowmen above a preoccupation with mere earthly things to contemplate the very essence of God.

It may seem that doctrinal exposition comprises much of the theological and devotional treatises. But theology for Law was never meant to be an end in itself. His systematic treatment of doctrine was foundational only. As Christopher Walton puts it:

He, as a wise master-builder, profoundly versed in the ancient science of spiritual architecture, which, by the way, seems to be almost lost, not only designs a noble edifice, complete in all its parts and perfect, but lays the basic broad and solid, upon the eternal "foundation that is laid," the rock Christ Jesus, and thence proceeds to raise the superstructure in due order and degree, according to the principles of science and his own practical experience . . . [;] he soberly proceeds with his labors until the top stone be put on, when, the whole being completed according to the Gospel model, he gives glory to God for his *free grace* in providing a ground or rock, so sure and steadfast, whereon to erect his edifice, with all the materials for its construction, and for enduing him with wisdom and strength and perseverance to complete it, though at the cost of all Worldly satisfactions. Such is a figurative representation of the ground of Mr. Law's understanding in his devotional writings.[38]

Even if one admits Law's heterodoxy on such subjects as God's wrath, one notes that he did not soften his views of God's justice as a palliative for the consciences of his convicted hearers. His beliefs grew from his own conviction of the nature of God. When Law says that through his teachings he hopes to magnify the "infinite merits" and "availing efficacy" of the passion of Christ, the sympathetic reader will hardly doubt his word. His scrupulous conscience would never allow him to stray far from the beaten path, even though his teachings may emit strange sounds at times. His head may err occasionally, but his heart never does. And Law, notwithstanding his appeal to the intellect, is first of all an apostle to the heart! Religion becomes to him subjective and emotional, while to most of his contemporaries it was historical and rational. His consuming passion is to propagate the life he knows among those who have not yet found it. He would inspire and lift men toward God. Any shortcoming on his part is purely an inadvertency. And someway men are willing to overlook apparent error when it may be compensated for by a warm spirit and pious intention. As R. M. Jones notes, it was Boehme's spiritual message and way of life that really interested Law, not his Theosophical ideas.[39]

VI *Letters and Addresses*

Written in 1731–1732 but not published until 1779, Law's three *Letters to a Lady Inclined to Enter the Communion of the Church of Rome* demonstrate his tender concern for one of his disciples who had inquired of him whether, in view of the schisms in the Protestant church and many signs of the church's defection from grace, it might be advisable for her to join the Catholic Church. Walton describes the woman's state of mind:

[She] had so bewildered herself in the labyrinth of polemical controversy concerning schisms and other ecclesiastical questions that her mind became filled with doubts of the sufficiency of God's grace in the ordinance of the established church of this country, of which she was a member, and perplexed about absolute decrees, the dispensations of providence, and other mysterious subjects.[40]

Law was quite restrained and tolerant in his answers, although he was not pro-Roman. He did not contend that any church had a monopoly on truth, but reminded the young woman that internal strife and spiritual inertness were not confined to any single religious body. At best, the church in the world is an imperfect institution, but it is the medium through which God chooses to communicate His will:

What is, therefore, left for us to do, madam, but to devote ourselves to such penitence, piety, and prayer, as the Heavenly Spirit of the Gospel requires of us; and to make the best use of the sacraments and institutions of Christ, that the present state of the church affordeth? We can neither stay in one communion, nor go into another, but we are in the same state, as to the Unity of the Church; every part is in a state of division, and chargeable with contributing to the cause of it.[41]

Law's advice to her was to "love the churches of Rome and Greece with the same affection and sense of Christian fellowship as she loved the Church of England." The pious tone and deep concern for spiritual well-being expressed in *Letters to a Lady* . . . illustrate Law's solicitude for many who sought his spiritual advice.

Two other works complete the later nondevotional list: *A Collection of Letters on the Most Interesting and Important Subjects* (1760) and *An Humble, Earnest, and Affectionate Address to the Clergy* (1761). The last-named, which was completed but a few days before his death, portrays Law's tender attitude toward young men in the ministry. He does not write about their professional duties, nor about books, nor even about sermonizing. Rather, he exhorts the young clergymen not to neglect the essential aspects of salvation. He also reiterates his earlier views upon Christian perfection as he points out:

The Pleader for Imperfection further supports himself by saying, No Man in the World, Christ excepted, was ever without Sin.—And so say I too; and with the Apostle I also add, "That if we say we have not Sinned, we make him a Liar."—But then it is as true to say, that we make *him a Liar*, if we deny the Possibility of our ever being freed from a Necessity of Sinning.[42]

Law's tone and manner here are devotional, but the work hardly merits a place alongside his major devotional writings because it dwells upon only a few devotional themes and is not so universally applicable. As he states at the outset of the work, "The Reason of my humbly and affectionately addressing this Discourse to the Clergy is . . . to invite and induce them . . . to the serious Perusal of . . . the *one Thing* needful. . . . It is the SPIRIT OF GOD brought again to his FIRST POWER OF LIFE IN US."[43]

The *Collection of Letters*, published posthumously by Thomas Langcake and George Ward, indeed contains a treasury of divine truths propounded by Law to various persons who counseled with him upon spiritual matters or who inquired concerning points of Boehme's doctrine. These twenty-five letters, written from King's Cliffe and later revised and edited by Law for publication, reflect the same pious spirit that pervades virtually everything he wrote, and insofar as they treat the universal themes that characterize devotional literature, they may belong to that genre. They are not treated as such here, however, as the letters are addressed more particularly to specific individual needs or are written in response to questions addressed to Law. They, therefore, constitute primarily personal advice, although they may be read for their general devotional admonition. The following excerpt is typical of the kind of spiritual advice that Law offers:

Only let your present and past Distress make you feel and acknowledge this twofold great Truth: *First*, That in and of yourself, you are nothing but Darkness, Vanity, and Misery; *Secondly*, that of yourself, you can no more help yourself to Light and Comfort, than you can create an Angel. People at all Times can seem to assent to these two Truths; but then it is an Assent that has no Depth or Reality, and so is of little or no Use: But your Condition has opened your Heart for a deep and full Conviction, and hold these two Truths, in the *same* Degree of Certainty as you know two and two to be four, and then you are with the *Prodigal come to yourself*, and above HALF YOUR WORK IS DONE.[44]

CHAPTER 4

The "Later" Law

I Mysticism and Jacob Boehme

THOSE who have called attention to Law's late introspective
tendencies have not always dissociated him from the mystical
extremists who have been suspect among religious thinkers generally.
In fact, most of the devotionalists of the past have much more of the
residue of mysticism in them than is commonly supposed. Before
praise or blame can be placed upon Law for his new emphasis it will
not be amiss to reexamine the essentials of mysticism and then
determine to what extent they are reflected in his later devotional
thought.

Unfortunately, "mysticism" has become for many an opprobrious
term frequently associated with occultism or fantastic views about
God and the world about us: necromancy, astrology, spiritualism. As
Caroline Spurgeon states, it is "a term so irresponsibly applied to
English that it has become the first duty of those who use it to explain
what they mean by it."[1] Another well-known source has said that
mysticism has been accused of "dealing in unsafe and presumptuous
speculation," or encouraging a sort of "extravagant, unhealthy,
hysterical self-hypnotism" or producing a "merely quasi-spiritual
feeling, vague, dreamy, and impractical."[2]

Perhaps, as Rufus Jones notes, mysticism has too often "staked its
realities upon what we call the subconscious."[3] Because the mystic is
convinced of the divine significance of his inner impressions, he may
assume wrongly that everything that springs out of the subconscious
is divinely given and he may fail to take into account the testimony of
reason and history. Obsessed with the thought that man may reach
God through intuition, he may neglect to guard against the capri-
ciousness that frequently attends a completely subjective experience.
Yet not all mystics deserve equally to be looked upon with suspicion,

for not all of them deviate far from "standard" religious doctrine and practice.

Ralph Inge, after surveying definitions by some twenty-six important writers and thinkers on mysticism, including Goethe, Canon Overton, Charles Kingsley, R. L. Nettleship, and Victor Cousin, offers his own synthesis: mysticism is "the attempt to realize, in thought and feeling, the immanence of the temporal in the eternal, and of the eternal in the temporal."[4] Inge sees ideal spiritual achievement, therefore, as consisting of supreme intimacy between the human and the Divine. This agrees substantially with a definition by another trusted authority on the subject: "Mysticism is the art of union with Reality. The mystic is a person who has attained that union in greater or less degree, or who aims at and believes in such attainment."[5]

Historian Henri Bremond defines mysticism as follows: "The essential phenomenon of mysticism is what is termed 'ecstasy,' a condition in which all communication with the exterior world is broken and the soul has consciousness that she is in communication with an interior object that is Infinite, Being, God."[6] Recently Gerald Bullett, speaking of the English mystics, says, "they are those men and women . . . who give the impression . . . that they have enjoyed contact and communion with something more real than is given in everyday human experience, an utterly indubitable quickening power, as it were a fountain of light and joy."[7]

Although mystical thinkers do not always concur in their avenues of approach to an Eternal Being, most of them agree that "unity underlies diversity." Wordsworth, for example, saw God through nature, as did Blake through the imagination. But the mystical mind is "founded upon an intuitive or experienced conviction of unity, of oneness, or alikeness in all things."[8] It believes that all phenomena about us are but manifestations of that underlying unity.

Man, of course, is capable of apprehending this underlying unity, for his spiritual faculty possesses a natural affinity for it. This inner knowledge, or intuitive perception of spiritual essence, constitutes for him the greatest reality. He is ever seeking to pierce through the outer manifestations into the true inner meaning of things. While the supreme or highest vision of God may be reserved for the elect few, mystics like Law assume that every person has something of the germ of mysticism in him and may participate in the mystical experience if he will undergo the disciplines that lead to it. Spurgeon agrees with William James that this longing on the part of so many to participate in the joys of mystical experience arises from a spark, or "mystical germ" which "makes response to their message."[9] This faculty, called variously "transcendental feeling," "imagination," "mystic reason," "cosmic consciousness," "Divine sagacity," "vision," shows the subject to be athirst for an "intimacy" with the Object of Longing.

The ascent up the hill of the mystical experience is not achieved without difficulty. As William Fleming, a religious historian, points out, "To be able to see God, man must partake himself of something God-like."[10] And since the aim of life is to become like God and at last to attain union with the Divine, life becomes for man "a continual advance, a ceaseless aspiration." Accordingly, the contemplative man must rise on the three rungs of the "ladder of perfection," that is, the "purgative," the "illuminative," and the "unitive."[11] The first phase involves contrition, confession, and amendment of life. It proceeds on the assumption that while man possesses the divine spark within himself, he must reckon with hindrances to spiritual attainment. Everything that would impede the upward progress of the soul must be purged. "Blessed are the pure in heart, for they shall see God" becomes the great rule of life.

The purgative life necessarily includes self-discipline, but it does not always mean the severe buffeting of the body as practiced by many hermits and medieval monks. As Inge points out, "Mysticism enjoins a dying life, not a living death."[12] Although mystics generally stress the severity of life, self-imposed rigor is not intended to be virtuous in itself; it is only to aid in preparing the way for spiritual illumination to follow.

The second state, or illuminative, stresses the inner life. Keenly aware of the new values he has discovered, the mystic understands the great relevance and meaning that the spiritual life has for him. Having rid himself of contaminating elements, he invites the full invasion of his inmost being by the supernatural, outside power.

The third stage, or unitive, is the highest known to man. In it the soul is joined to God; man beholds God face to face. Although, as Inge reminds us, complete union with God is "the ideal limit of religion, the attainment . . . would be at once its consummation and annihilation. It is in the continual but unending approximation to it that the life of religion subsists."[13] In other words, there is nothing static about even the highest point in the mystical experience; man is expected to press ever higher, for an Infinite Being can never be fully comprehended by the contemplative mind. This high stage, however, is frequented by unusual manifestations to the consciousness. Many mystics looked for ecstatic revelations, trances, or visions, described as "a state of inward sensation or knowledge . . . that supervened at times during the third stage."[14] The ecstasy was a foretaste of the Divine. It was indescribable. Eternity was manifesting itself in time. It was realization of a world in which all is God and God is all:

Ecstasy or vision begins when thought ceases, to our consciousness, to proceed from ourselves. It differs from dreaming, because the subject is awake. It differs from hallucination, because there is no organic disturbance: it is, or claims to be, a temporary enhancement, not a partial disintegration, of the mental faculties. Lastly, it differs from poetical inspiration, because the imagination is passive.[15]

William James depicts the highest mystical state by ascribing to it four descriptive qualities: (1) ineffable, i.e., no adequate report can be given of it in words; (2) noetic, or it provides deep insights into truth; (3) transient, it cannot be sustained for long; (4) passive, or after the preliminary preparation, the mystic is held by a superior power.[16]

That such psychical phenomena have actually been experienced is hardly open to doubt. However, to consider them as an essential part of mysticism is, as Inge contends, to mix strange "Asiatic leaven" with "Alexandrine thought." The great spiritual masters usually attach minor importance to them. "As a rule, visions were regarded as special rewards bestowed by the goodness of God on the struggling saint, and especially on the beginner, to refresh and strengthen him in the hour of need."[17] According to Inge, Plotinus believed himself to have had the "beatific vision" four times while Porphry was his disciple; Porphry himself had it once. The later Neo-Platonists came to believe it was not to be experienced in this world. Eckhart and other Christian mystics did not stress it. Ascetic mystics, or those confined to the cloister, seem to have participated in it more frequently. In other words, the mystic seldom appealed to these "peak" experiences. He would more often speak of the superiority of reason, by which he meant, in the manner of the Cambridge Platonists, the logic of the whole personality.

For the most part, the more favorably received mystics of the past have been inclined to treat man as an entity made up of intellect, temperament, and will. Where they have not insisted upon the validity of one of these aspects of man's personality to the exclusion of the others, they have usually avoided the objectionable beliefs that have so often heaped reproach upon their way of life.

The term "mysticism," therefore, admits a variety of connotations.

However, the intuitive approach to reality, the awareness of unity in diversity, the passion to know the spiritual reality which underlies and unifies all things, all characterize mysticism wherever it is found. And J. B. Green, a critic of Law's mystical tendencies, comments significantly that there is something in mysticism toward which every religious person ought to aspire: union with God, which lies at the root of all religious devotion.[18]

Recently Stephen Hobhouse has helped to revise Overton's estimate of mystical influences upon Law. He mentions the fourteenth-century school of Meister Eckhart, comprised of Johannes Tauler, Henry Suso, Jan Van Ruysbroeck, and the author of *Theologia Germanica*, as exerting a more powerful influence than is commonly recognized. Among other writers to whom Law occasionally refers are St. Augustine, Dionysius the Areopagite, Origen, and Irenaeus.[19] Law's debt to Boehme is admittedly great, but one has first to recognize the latter's own remarks concerning those who influenced him. Francis Okeley's words come readily to mind when he describes Law as "a mystical bee . . . whose works are like so many honey-combs by him assiduously collected, formed, digested, and filled during a long life of all the spiritual writers or mystic flowers, ancient and modern."[20]

In his second reply to Dr. Trapp, Law comments, speaking of Trapp's criticism of his lack of appreciation of Virgil, Terence, and Horace:

Had the Doctor been more conversant in the Writings of a Set of men called *Mystical Divines*, than he appears to have been, he had been better able to have charged me with *humble Plagiary* than he is at present . . . Of these Mystical Divines I thank God I have been a diligent Reader, through all Ages of the Church, from the Apostolical *Dionysius the Areopagite*, down to the great *Fenelon*, Archbishop of Cambrai, the illuminated *Guyon*, and *M. Bertot.* . . . But I apprehend the Doctor to be as great a Stranger to the Writers of this kind, with which every Age of the Church has been blessed, and to know no more of the Divine *Ruysbroeck, Tauler, Suso, Harphius, Johannes de Cruce*, etc., than he does of *J. B.*[21]

Law's disinclination to speak of his debt to other writers, together with his disposition to assimilate what he read before setting it forth as his own, increases the difficulty of confirming debt. The presence of hundreds of books in the King's Cliffe Library suggests that Law read widely, but parallels between his thought and that of other writers do not always establish influence.

One can see how St. Augustine's emphasis upon the will and the virtues of humility and love would find ready response in Law. Similarly, Dionysius the Areopagite's fourth treatise on mystical theology, insisting upon the mystical union with the Creator, and Johannes Tauler's stress upon the spark of God in the soul would be a natural part of Law's mystical thought. Jan Van Ruysbroeck's highly intuitive approach to truth and his strong and disciplined intellect, together with his absorption in God, are typical of Law. The expressions of Christian thinkers, however, are not always used because they are traditional or borrowed, but because they fit human experience. As Hobhouse notes, there are certain broad areas of mystical expression, and coincidence of language is an unsafe guide to influence. One can find parallel passages from Law and Oriental writers whom he could not possibly have read. His thought has been at times confused with that of Meister Eckhart because of certain parallel passages; however, it is not known that he actually read Eckhart's writings. One may assume that the commonality of experience expressed by the mystics spoke on occasion to Law through the writers whom he consulted. But, with one major exception, his language becomes primarily his own.

The greatest single mystical influence, of course, is that of Jacob Boehme, whose works Law was studying in the original German between 1740 and the publication of *The Spirit of Prayer*. Law mentions Boehme more frequently than any other writer as "a Guide to the Truth of all The Mysteries of the Kingdom of God."[22]

Walton gives the following account of Law's introduction to Boehme's works by a friend:

In an intimate interview I had with Mr. Law a few months before his decease . . . I inquired of him when and how he first met with Behmen's works. He replied . . . the first notice he had of him was from a treatise called "Fides et Ratio," published at Amsterdam, 1707. . . . "When I first began to read him," says he, "he put me into a perfect sweat."[23]

Always a sensitive and devout young man, Boehme was disturbed by the disunity of Protestantism. Upon several occasions he professed to see supernatural manifestations and to hear mysteriously divine injunctions. Well-known to all Boehme readers is the account of his vision one day from watching the sun's reflections from a bright pewter dish. He felt that the light allowed him to see beneath appearances into the inner meaning of all phenomena. The vision continued for a time, and he was enabled thereby to analyze the inner properties of all things in nature. Later on, when he received a similar vision, he decided to write his experiences for the benefit of others.[24]

Reading Jacob Boehme may give the initial impression that he is concerned more with cosmology than with theology, but a look at the range of his subjects reveals that his interests really centered upon theological belief and devotional activity.[25] Law found him to be one of those rare mystics who professed to have experienced a direct vision of God and who wrote at length upon nature and the meaning of the world simply because he was dissatisfied with the currently accepted oversimplifications upon these subjects. Impatient of the labels and dogmas commonly associated with God and religion, Boehme attempted to give a faithful description of the spiritual goals that he believed man ought to envision and strive for. He believed that communication of the insights he had received would aid man in his quest for higher spiritual attainment. Law was strengthened and inspired in his own devotional writings by the spiritual ardor that suffused the thought of this German mystic.

Of course, not all of the complexities of mysticism are reflected in William Law's works, but correspondences between the basic beliefs of Boehme and Law become apparent at once. For instance, as a critic of Boehme, John Stoudt, points out, Boehme's problem was that of the divided self. Originally man was made in the spiritual image of God and enjoyed perfect communion with Him. However, ignorantly man sought separation from God and fell, as a result, into discord and misery. Boehme tried to resolve the disunity between God and man and to teach the final victory of God's Kingdom through a spiritual rebirth in the human heart. Law also emphasized the place of regeneration in resolving the disharmony which he saw in man's nature. Boehme's emphasis upon the experience of unity as the *summum bonum* of existence accounts for his long disquisitions upon union with God rather than foreign spirit forces. Likewise, Law belongs to the tradition of Christian mystics who taught the need for achieving unity through restoration of corrupted nature to the image of God from which man had fallen.

Stoudt also says that Boehme did away with the "climbing of the ladder" concept in approaching God.[26] That is, he believed that God was near and, without waiting for the soul's gradual ascent, would invade it whenever it was prepared. In seeking for the union of the will of man with the will of God, however, both Boehme and Law emphasize the "orientation of our wills to God" as needful preparation for the invasion of the soul by the Spirit. The place of the will assumes primary importance in the thinking of both men.

Probably the essential merit of Boehme's influence lies in its "clear teaching as to the nature of true regeneration and the true Christian life." The important problem for Boehme was the study of the divine life in both macrocosm and microcosm. Law was confident that a full review of the history of the atonement and its far-reaching implications would give to man a better appreciation of his spiritual heritage and sensitize his spirit to the deep-seated ways in which God works upon human nature. Law was not content with merely a hurried summary of man's Adamic perfection, his defection from grace, and his spiritual renovation. He was intrigued with the whole process of spiritual recovery and believed man's salvation depended in part upon his exploring in some intellectual detail what salvation required. Although Anglican theology was for Law a settled, coherent system, as his debate with Hoadley revealed earlier, J.B. Green points out that Law saw that system "posited against a background which cried out for more profound explanations."[27]

That Law agreed with the principal convictions of the mystics can hardly be disputed: emphasis upon the need for purging of the inner nature from moral defilement, the intuitive perception of spirituality which underlies and unifies all things, and aspiration toward union with God. But it is also necessary to recognize these variations in Law's thought: (1) He never identified himself deliberately with any school of mystics; neither did he lay claim to the "peaks" of ecstasy which were professed by the visionaries. (2) When he became a devotee of Boehme, Law recanted nothing that he wrote in his early period; neither did his reverence for Scripture openly diminish. (3) An intense devotional spirit still possessed him in the late works; in fact, his passion to know God increased. One may note an alteration of the currents in some of his writings, but one is never conscious that new influences brought about new aims on his part or banished old ones. (4) Law chose to restate doctrines as they were formulated by other men rather than create novel doctrines of his own.

Contending that Law's writings under the influence of Boehme show that the former's knowledge and experience were derivative, Arthur Hopkinson, a critic of Law's thought, doubts whether, in the strictest sense, Law may be classed as a mystic at all. According to Hopkinson, a true mystic possesses a faculty that merges the human with the divine: "It [the mystic faculty] is more than earnest and ordered devotion; it involves a completeness of spiritual sympathy, a stretching out into the ineffable."[28] There is bound to be a difference, then, between the mystical experience that one gets through second-hand knowledge and that which results from firsthand mystical revelation. Knowing *about* mysticism and *being* a mystic are two different things.

In any case, by his own admission, Law allowed the thought of Jacob Boehme and others to permeate his own views of God, man, and the universe, and the result is at least a shift of emphases and a realignment of perspectives.

Whatever may be said of the change in Law's thought with the advent of the pronounced mystical note, the new emphasis provided no deterrent to the same devotional impulse that pervaded *Christian Perfection* and *A Serious Call.* As Hopkinson reminds us, "At most Behmen helped to bring to a flame the smoldering devotion of a man in many ways greater than himself."[29] One still discerns the persistent stress upon fashioning of one's life and thought to secure divine approval and preoccupation with ways and means of conforming to the divine image as the all-important business of life. One notes also the patient enjoining of the life of devotion upon everybody, as Aldous Huxley states, "—for the congenitally active and devotional no less than for the congenitally contemplative." If, as Overton asserts, "the complete union of the soul with God" is the goal of all mysticism, then Law does not fail to continue striving toward that end with warmly devotional appeal.

II   *Later Works of Devotion:* The Spirit of Prayer,
The Spirit of Love, *and* The Way to Divine Knowledge

If Law alienated such contemporary disciples as John and Charles Wesley through his mystical predilections, his work was later to receive many contemporary plaudits from such devotees as Canon Overton, Alexander Whyte, and W. R. Inge. The latter speaks of *The Spirit of Love* and *The Spirit of Prayer* as the "two most charming of Law's mystical works," the latter work deserving claim as his masterpiece. Christopher Walton lavishly contends that "Law's readers will rise up from those books saying, 'these are the two best books in the world.'" And Whyte says no less enthusiastically, "The intellectual and experimental range of *The Spirit of Prayer* and *The Spirit of Love* is much more extended and profound than is the range of what is popularly known as orthodox and evangelical doctrine."[30] Some have claimed that Law's embracing of Boehme's thought gives evidence of his freedom from sectarianism and narrowmindedness.

Mere praise or censure of his mystical writings does not alter the fact that *The Spirit of Love, The Spirit of Prayer*, and *The Way to Divine Knowledge* are the works upon which Law spent his most strenuous efforts and about which he felt most deeply. In them one discerns his incandescent ardor as he portrays a spirituality in which love is dominant. These works are primarily devotional, for they seek above everything else to direct the soul to pious living. The principal task here will be to point out the devotional themes, to note significant variations in Law's thought under mystical influences, and to estimate what bearing his shift in emphasis had upon his devotional appeal.

The Spirit of Prayer reiterates that prayer is more than petition; it is synonymous with a *life* of devotion. Desiring to communicate his goodness, God created man in the divine image. Through the fall from the celestial state man was cut off from divine life. The whole of religion speaks of how Jesus Christ, by the giving of his life, effected a regeneration or new life. With the unfolding of the Trinity in fallen Adam, the spark of divinity still in man reaches for the salvation offered him. Dialogues between Academicus, Rusticus, Theophilus, Humanus treat of the exact nature of the fall and how the heart of man pants for God continually rather than merely spending specified times in prayer. The religion of mere reason is folly. The spirit of prayer is exemplified in penitence, thanksgiving, and new life in God.

Originally prepared as an introduction to a new edition of Boehme's works, *The Way to Divine Knowledge* forms three dialogues as a continuation of *The Spirit of Prayer*. It continues to set forth the major proof of Christianity as its spiritual life and stresses the importance of free will as "the power by which a man gives himself up to anything." Reason, properly employed, is a valuable aid to religion, but faith is paramount. The discussion of the seven properties of nature again harks back to Boehme's doctrine, but the emphasis here is upon the fourth property where mystical light breaks forth in man and the new birth becomes a brilliant reality.

The Spirit of Love takes the form of a letter to a friend who has been deeply affected by the spirit in Law's writings. He questions whether the ideal of love extolled was too impractical and whether a Being who was all love was contrary to Scripture, which described God as a god of righteousness and judgment. The answer forms the substance of this treatise.

The Spirit of Love's underlying presupposition is that God is an inevitable will to all goodness. Happiness and goodness proceed from Him naturally, for He has nothing else to give. He wills only to manifest Himself to everything that wants Him. Considerable space is given to Boehme's doctrine of the properties of nature, where the work of fire is primary. The dialogue turns on the doctrine of the atonement and its purpose to remove the wrath between God and man. Christ had done this by giving His life. Election, contrary to the Calvinist belief, consists in man's assertion of will to receive new light, which God has already elected for him. With the infusion of that life, all self, composed of covetousness, pride, and wrath—the hell in his nature—is abolished and restoration between man God is effected.

Here the mystical accretions of Boehme's theology are in greater abundance. Increasingly intrigued by the German mystic's elaborate embroidery of the doctrines of Creation, Fall, and Redemption, Law offered freely to his readers the plausible subtleties that had fired his own imagination and deepened his own spiritual ardor.

III   *Union-with-God Theme*

Writing under the mystical influence, Law quite naturally gave the union-with-God theme greater prominence than in the early devotional works. To desire union with Christ at all times, in all places; to hope that tempers of the inner life may be changed "into the Spirit and Temper of the Holy Jesus" becomes the essence of religion for him. As he wrote in *The Spirit of Prayer*,

Wherever thou goest, whatever thou dost, at Home or Abroad, or at Church, do all in a Desire of Union with Christ, in Imitation of his Tempers and Inclinations, and look upon all as Nothing, but that which exercises, and increases the Spirit and Life of Christ in thy Soul. From Morning to Night keep Jesus in thy Heart, long for Nothing, desire Nothing, hope for Nothing, but to have all that is within Thee changed into the Spirit and Temper of the Holy Jesus.[31]

Law's insistence upon the unitive experience with God may be found frequently in *The Spirit of Prayer*: "For the Heart is always far from God, unless the Spirit of Christ be alive in it. . . . And thus the Work of our Salvation is wholly and solely the Work of the Light and Spirit of God, dwelling and operating in us."

The Spirit of Love abounds with similar statements: "For Nature and Creature, without the Christ of God, or the Divine Life in Union with it, is and can be nothing else but this mere *Emptiness, Hunger* and *Want* of all that which can alone make it good and happy."[32] Again from *The Spirit of Love*:

And thus . . . you have the fullest Proof in *what* your Salvation precisely consists. Not in any historic Faith, or Knowledge of any Thing absent or distant from you, not in any Variety of Restraints, Rules, and Methods of practicing Virtues, not in any *Formality* of Opinion about *Faith* and *Works, Repentance, Forgiveness* of *Sins*, or *Justification*, and *Sanctification*, not in any Truth, or Righteousness, that you can have from yourself, from the best of Men or Books, but wholly and solely in the *Life of God*, or Christ of God *quickened* and born again in you, or, in other Words, in the Restoration and perfect Union of the *twofold Life* in the Humanity.[33]

The theme continues in *The Way to Divine Knowledge*: "This is the true and only Ground of Religion; viz., to alter our State of Existence *in God*, and to have more of the Divine Nature and Perfections communicated to us . . . and puts us in Possession of *something* of God. . . . Everything that is in Life, has its Degree of Life in and from God; it lives and moves and has its Being in God."[34]

The union-with-God theme is one of Law's favorites, for it gives him an opportunity to rehearse at length how God has exemplified his love for man in the elaborate language of Boehme. God created the world out of love and a desire to have children in His likeness. Man is the microcosm consisting of soul, body, and spirit. God is the deepest ground, the life-giving root of all existence. God and Christ, heaven and hell, life and death are in every human heart. If one offers his heart willfully to God, then he becomes one with God and Paradise is his. Down deep in the heart, therefore, are the seeds of Divine Life. Sin has made the inner life dark, and self-love, pride, and envy rule unless the will turns toward reunion with the Light of God:

Eternal Beings have but *one Life* and *one Good*, and that is the Life of God. The Spirit of the Soul is in itself nothing else but a Spirit breathed forth from the Life of God, and for this only End, that the Life of God, the Nature of God, the Working of God, the Tempers of God, might be manifested in it.[35]

Eusebius, one of the characters in *The Spirit of Love*, comments:

. . . all salvation is, and can be nothing else, but the *Manifestation* of the Life of God in the Soul. How clearly does this give the solid Distinction between

inward Holiness, and all outward, creaturely Practices. All that God has
done for Man by any particular Dispensations, whether by the *Law*, or the
Prophets, by the *Scriptures*, or *Ordinances* of the *Church*, are only as Helps
to an Holiness which they cannot give. . . .[36]

Similarly, in *The Way to Divine Knowledge*:

This is Christian Redemption; on the one side, it is the *Heavenly Divine
Life offering itself again to the inward Man, that has lost it.* On the other side,
it is the *Hope, the Faith, and Desire of this inward Man, hungering, and
thirsting, stretching after, and calling upon this Divine and Heavenly Life.*[37]

Similar extolling of subjective experience also may be noted in
such devotional mystical writers as Jan Van Ruysbroeck and
Dionysius the Areopagite—whom Law presumably read. Dionysius
said, "Unity of heart is a bond which draws together body and soul,
heart and senses, and all the outward and inward powers and encloses
them in the union of love. . . ." Inwardness means that a man is
turned within his own heart, and thereby he may understand and feel
the interior workings and the interior words of God.[38] This mystical
inclination to dwell upon inner reality is prompted by the conviction
that each individual may know God personally and vitally and looks
forward to spiritual union as the highest achievement of that
experience.

The idea of God's birth in the depths of man's soul is the aim of all
mystical practice. What Bernard of Clairvaux called "spark" and
Suso, Tauler, and the author of *Theologia Germanica* called
"ground" of the soul was the point where the forces of the soul
converged to produce piety. Here God imparts himself to man in an
inexplicable manner. St. Augustine traced his beginning of the
Divine Life to the new birth of God within.

IV   *Models of Perfection Theme*

Emulation of the life of Christ as an important step in achieving a
life of perfection, which was so forcefully stressed in Law's early
works, receives attention in the later works also. The exhortations are
at times more implicit than formerly, but they are too prominent to be
overlooked. When one reflects upon the doctrine of the atonement as
held by Law, in which the efficacy of the life of Christ is emphasized
more than the death, one is not surprised to see him urge the teachings
and example of the Lord as fundamental to a union with the Divine

Life. In fact, the devotional warmth becomes more pronounced where he urges the believer to participate in the Divine Life held before him:

> ... In all Respects we are as *strictly*, as *intimately* connected with, and related to Him as the *one Redeemer*, as we are to *Adam* as the *one Father* of all Mankind. So that Christ by his Sufferings and Death become [*sic*] in all of us our Wisdom, our Righteousness, our Justification and Redemption, is the same sober and solid Truth, as *Adam* by his Fall become [*sic*] in all of us our Foolishness, our Impurity, our Corruption and Death.[30]

The veneration in which Law continues to hold the teachings of Scripture is also too pronounced to ignore in the later treatises. Those who are repelled by the prolix expository digressions may at first be inclined to think he has subverted the Scriptures to the mazes of Behmenistic doctrine. But Law is steadfast in his commitments to biblical language. He is never so preoccupied with metaphysical subtleties that he abandons conventional religious practices and beliefs. Whatever he says to explain the implications of the mystical doctrines is always meant to enhance the scriptural view, not to replace it. Even when he praises the far-fetched theorizing of Jacob Boehme upon the Scriptures, it is not with the thought that he has discovered a new doctrine; rather it is to point out that Boehme's work is to make plain truths already held.[40]

Illustration of Law's continued respect for the Scriptures as the basis for achieving perfection may be noted in the following selection from the later devotional works:

> ... Christians have nothing to excuse their wandering from the One great Point, since both the Testaments bear so open a Witness to it. "In the day that thou eatest thereof, thou shalt surely die," says the Old Testament. "Except a man be born again from above, of the Word and Spirit of God, he cannot enter into the Kingdom of Heaven," says the New Testament.[41]

Theogenes says, "And thus, Sir, all the Treasures of the Wisdom and Goodness of God, hidden in the Letter of Scripture, made the Comfort and Delight of my Soul ... till all Evil shall be extinguished, and all Disorder go back again to its first harmonious State of Perfection."[42]

Whatever one may think of the use that Law made of the Bible in his later devotional period, he must always admit, as has been pointed out repeatedly here, that Law never willfully departed from scriptural authority. Whatever he may have accepted from the system of Jacob Boehme, or anyone else, was meant only to supplement the biblical record, not to replace it. Law emphasizes the point very late in *The Spirit of Love* when he alludes to the scriptural exposition of the nature of the atonement; in addition, he refers to Christ as the unimpeachable authority for our mode of conduct here. In exhorting his friend to assert his faith and resign himself to the ways of God, Theophilus says, "If you distrust my Words, hear the Words of Christ himself: 'Learn of me,' says He, 'for I am meek and lowly of Heart, and ye shall find Rest to your Souls.'"[43]

V   *Theme of Self-Denial*

Insistence upon self-denial as a means for attaining to the spiritual life, another key devotional theme, also assumes prominence in the later writings of Law. As has been noted, the mystics view the first steps toward union with God as consisting in recognizing the futility of life, the nothingness of human existence. Even Buddhism and other Indian mysticisms are rooted in the experience of the illusoriness of all earthly things.

The author of *Theologia Germanica*, in teaching that man must forsake all things in the manner of Christ and pursue a selfless life, says,

Now in this temporal world, man stands between heaven and hell and can turn himself to which of these he will. For the more of own, the more of hell and bale, and the less of self-will, the less of hell and the nearer to heaven. . . . He who has or wills aught of his own, is himself owned, and he who has and wills naught of his own, and desires to have naught, is quit and free and owned of naught.[44]

Fenelon also was most insistent upon the disparagement of the human will if one is to achieve a perfect spiritual state. "This death to ourselves, and all that we love, which is general and superficial in our will, when we have pierced it . . . will penetrate to the center. It will leave nothing to the creature. It will push out, relentlessly, all that is not good."[45] Jan Van Ruysbroeck declared similarly, "The forsaking of one's own will causes a man to live without preference for either this or that . . . in those things which are strange and special in the saints. . . . It makes him live always according to the glory and the commandments of God."[46]

The later writings of Law lay as much stress upon self-renunciation as a means for spiritual betterment as *Christian Perfection* and *A Serious Call.* A typical passage follows:

But Christ cannot be thy Power and thy Life, till in Obedience to his Call, *thou deniest thyself, takest up thy daily Cross, and followest Him,* in the Regeneration. This is peremptory, it admits of no Reserve or Evasion, it is the one Way to Christ and Eternal Life. But be where thou wilt, either *here,* or at *Rome,* or *Geneva,* if *Self* is undenied, if thou livest to thine *own Will,* to the Pleasures of thy natural Lust and Appetites, Senses and Passions, and in Conformity to the vain Customs, and Spirit of this World, thou art dead whilst thou livest. . . .[47]

In fact, the new life can only come about after the self-life is dead and Christ's own life is formed in the believer. The spirit of love and the spirit of prayer and the way to divine knowledge are essentially the same thing: new life created in place of the old. And before new life can be brought forth, one must ruthlessly abnegate self. That Law makes this point central is seen when he says, "But when we once apprehend but in some good Degree, the *All* of God, and the *Nothingness* of ourselves, we have got a Truth, whose Usefulness and Benefit no Words can express."[48] He says further, "Now *Self* is all that you have, it is your sole Possession; you have no Goods of your *own,* nothing is yours but *this Self.* The Riches of *Self* are your *own Riches;* but *all this Self* is to be parted with before the Pearl is yours."

In *The Way to Divine Knowledge* the same theme continues to be dominant:

This is the simple Nature, and sole Drift of the Gospel; it means no more than making known to Man that this World, and the Life of it, is his Fall, and Separation from God, and Happiness . . . can only be obtained by renouncing all Love, and Adherence to the Things of this World. . . .

To embrace the Gospel, is to enter with all our Hearts into its Terms of dying to all that is earthly both within us, and without us. . . .[49]

Theophilus says to Academicus, "You are to turn wholly from yourself, and to give up yourself wholly unto God . . . ," and then outlines a fitting prayer which will lead to that life:

Oh my God, with all the Strength of my Soul, assisted by thy Grace, I desire and resolve to resist and deny all my own Will, earthly Tempers, selfish Views, and Inclinations; everything that the Spirit of this World, and the

Vanity of fallen Nature, prompts me to. I give myself up wholly and solely unto Thee, to be all thine, to have, and do, and be, inwardly and outwardly, according to thy good Pleasure. I desire to live for no other Ends, with no other Designs, but to accomplish the Work which thou requirest of me, an humble, obedient, faithful, thankful Instrument in thy Hands to be used as thou pleasest.[50]

VI   Theme of Prayer

The later works of Law continue to touch upon prayer as a vital part of man's life with God—one of the popular themes in the devotional tradition. The accent shifts somewhat from the special times and subjects of prayer noted in *A Serious Call* to an all-embracing spirit of prayer which man may possess at all times. This is not to imply that man is a self-contained being who has no need to call upon divine help. The following summary of the main tenets in Law's later teaching upon this point makes quite clear that spiritual life must derive originally from an outside source:

1. He [man] is the son of a fallen Angel. 2. He is the Son of a Male and Female of this bestial World. 3. He is a Son of the Lamb of God, and has a Birth of Heaven again in his Soul. Hence we see also, that all we have to fear, to hate, and renounce; all that we have to love, to desire, and pray for is *all within ourselves.*[51]

Rusticus now propounds to Academicus the heart of the matter: "The *Spirit of Prayer*" is a "*State* of the Heart" which has become the "*governing* Principle of the Soul's Life . . . And if it is a living State of the Heart, must it not have its Life in itself, independent of every outward Time and Occasion?"[52] Law is simply saying that man's recovery of the lost image of God consists of a prayerful, inner-searching for the spirit which is available at all times. As he puts it summarily in *The Way to Divine Knowledge*:

This is Christian Redemption; on the one side, *it is the Heavenly Divine Life offering itself again to the inward Man, that had lost it.* On the other side, it is the *Hope, the Faith, and Desire of this inward Man, hungering, and thirsting, stretching after, and calling upon this Divine and Heavenly Life.*[53]

And in *The Spirit of Prayer*:

For this turning to God according to the inward *Feeling, Want,* and

Motion of your own Heart, in Love, in Trust, in Faith of having from him all that you want, and wish to have, this turning thus unto God, whether it be with, or without Words, is the best Form of Prayer in the World.[54]

Law has not modified drastically his former beliefs about prayer. His emphasis has merely shifted more noticeably from acts of prayer to a condition of life. As one goes back to reread *Christian Perfection* and *A Serious Call*, he finds that Law held this belief in embryo even there. A careful reading of *The Spirit of Prayer, The Spirit of Love*, and *The Way to Divine Knowledge* shows that Law never repudiates "times and hours of prayer," but wishes rather that the pious supplicant might progress beyond these to speak forth "Spirit and Life and Love towards God." Moreover, he makes it plain that he does not oppose formal prayers: "I should be so far from cen- suring . . . a *Formality* of Prayer, that I should say, Blessed and happy are they, whose Hearts are tied to . . . a Form of Words. It is not therefore, Sir, a set Form of Words that is spoken against, but an *heartless* Form, a Form that has no Relation to, or Correspondence with, the State of the Heart that uses it."[55]

This remarkably refined conception of the centrality of true devotion, which is hardly typical of the religious temper of the early eighteenth century, denotes a clear understanding of what is involved in living a spiritual life. Law makes no concessions to the worldly spirit. To him, the most insidious threat to a transformed life in the world is not doctrinal heresy, but is rather succumbing to the daily temptations to conform to the spirit of the world.

The manuals of Christian devotion during the medieval and Renaissance periods stressed the forms of prayer. Reflections and meditations usually preceded or accompanied the overt act, but the ascent of the soul to God was invariably through the formulated prayer contained in the Prayer Book or manual of private devotion. But Law envisions far more. He addresses himself to the whole range of man's spiritual dilemma. Refusing to oversimplify or gloss over the problems that man faces, he carefully analyzes all that occurred to the human race as a result of original sin and reconstructs the series of steps necessary for restoration. He reasons that no human effort is sufficient to bridge the gap between fallen man and his pristine status; hence one sees the emphasis on the supreme role of Deity in effecting a reconciliation. Since man's quest is to regain the status from which he has fallen, prayer is treated as a human spirit rising once more to God, as sweet incense. But

. . . this Spirit of Prayer is not to be taught you by a Book, or brought into you by an *Art* from without, but must be an inward Birth, that must arise from your own *Fire* and *Light* within you, as the Air arises from the Fire and Light of this World.[56]

The Neo-Platonic doctrine of emanation, or the belief that the world was a spontaneous effluence from God Himself, which was held by both Law and Boehme, although objected to by many churchmen, leads logically to another aspect of Law's theory of prayer as rising within the heart. This belief was simply that man came out from God in whom he had existed from all eternity; therefore, if the soul is to be reunited with its natural habitat, it will probably do so from an inner drive, or act of the will. This belief recognizes the need for an inner compulsion to will a reunion with the divine element. Hence the final emphasis in *The Spirit of Prayer* upon "feeling" and "desire." One sees clearly what Law means when he says, "My own good Spirit is the Breath of God in me, and so related to God, as the Breath of my animal Life is related to the *Air*, or Spirit of this outward World."

The result for the worshiper will be a happy one. No vice can harbor within; no infirmity can take root; and praying will become as natural as breathing. The Holy Spirit, or the "breath of eternity," has its "seed of life" in the soul, and the spiritual victory which finally ensues becomes the triumph of the Kingdom of God within. Such a state is the "sublime," the "exalted," the "angelic."

VII   *Elaborations upon Cosmology and Axiology*

Many devotional writers have speculated upon the nature of man and the makeup of the world, but rarely does one encounter cosmology as a pervasive, integral part of devotional thought as much as in Law. The main business of his life was to apprehend God and His world. He attempts to know the Triune God and in his similitude the whole of creation. He represents the Father as the underlying essence of the universe, described as "fire," or "restless energy." The Son expresses "the illumination of the love which ever flows from the Divine essence," and the Holy Spirit, somewhat less distinctly defined, represents the "love-light of the Christ within." Correspondingly, man's personality is conceived as a composite of fire, light, and air. When sin enters man, it deprives him of the light of Christ and the Holy Spirit, but not of the fire-substance of the Creator.

By his own admission, Law was impressed by Jacob Boehme's living intuition of nature and his regarding of the universe as a total organism of which man is the microcosm. Boehme may have received his inspiration from such sources as the Jewish Kabbala, or the philosophy of Philo of Alexandria, or the whole group of German mystics: Eckhart, Tauler, Suso, and the author of *Theologia Germanica*. But Law's interpolations of theory of the makeup of man and the world are evidence of an imaginative attempt to explore the mysterious and to supply a full-orbed account of the divine process.

After accepting the literal biblical account of the creation and fall, Law recognized that the written record gave only the barest outlines of what actually took place. The silence of Revelation about many matters that intrigued him challenged him to cast about for an adequate myth to satisfy his deep query. Since understanding the implications of dogma was always regarded by Law as essential to spiritual edification, he theorized elaborately about the meaning of biblical language. Properly understood, these expositions of the nature of Christianity and meaning of Christian doctrine were intended to attract the reader to a deeper sense of piety by inspiring in him a sense of awe and reverence.

Sensing the need for communicating his convictions to his readers, Law resorts increasingly to long discussions of man's origin, the nature of sin and regeneration as though he would anticipate and answer in advance any question that might arise among those who were unfamiliar with his thought. No intricacy about man's relationship to God and the world is too detailed for him to explore. When Law talks about "correct thinking" in *The Spirit of Love* and *The Spirit of Prayer*, he is thinking of its importance as a spiritual exercise. One must possess the "right" perspective and take the "correct" view of nature, God, and himself. He must know where to look for divine aid and be sensitive to the possibilities of discovering God within himself. A great deal depends upon his awareness of the spiritual possibilities, which can come about only after he has considered aright his status as one alienated from the life of God—as one who needs to realign both his thinking and method of approach to spiritual problems. Edification can result only when the mind has pushed out beyond the horizons of accepted teachings into the mysteries of the cosmos and ramifications of Christian doctrine.

The Way to Divine Knowledge also emphasizes the point that all knowledge that is not concerned with divine matters is not true knowledge. To relate oneself properly to God, one ought to inquire seriously into cosmology and axiology in an attempt to fathom some of the mysteries of God, for a study of the origin of the world, the original state of man, and the nature of the fall will help man to appreciate what God has done for him and engender thereby a sense of righteousness. Discussion of theological points, then, in the devotional writings, becomes an integral part of the devotional reading. In all of this there is a remarkable absence of doctrinal dispute or argument for its own sake. Law seems to assume that the inquiring heart has laid down its arms of incredulity and seeks only to know how to find the right way to worship.

It must be admitted that when Law resorted to the teachings of the mystics for explications of his doctrines, some readers parted company with him.[57] Perhaps he was in error to presume that a rationale for religion perfectly acceptable to him would also be intellectually acceptable to others. Undoubtedly he made his doctrine less popular by spinning out so elaborately the intricacies of his belief. Yet here again, as in *Christian Perfection* and *A Serious Call*, Law believed with the Cambridge Platonists that piety begins with intellectual inquiry and that the first act of worship must therefore consist in a right apprehension of the nature of God and the universe and man's relation to them. In all of this, Law never falters in his devotional intent. As Hopkinson puts it, "Law did not cease to be devotional when he became a mystic."[58]

Law's emulation of Boehme's long preambles and detailed expositions to theological statements and devotional admonitions is unique in the tradition of devotional prose. These discourses upon the rationale and intricacies of the Christian faith may at times tax the patience of the general reader, even though the devotional intent is unquestioned. Theophilus, for example, becomes Law's spokesman for a prolix exposition of the nature of the fall and its implications for man and the means of restoration, together with a rationale for man's devotional life in the world. The second dialogue in *The Spirit of Prayer* veers into a long discourse upon Adam's original perfection and the effect of his fall. While much that one encounters here agrees with that taught by Thomas à Kempis, Richard Baxter, and others in the devotional tradition, the abstruse manner may at times obscure the devotional purpose. The following passage may strike one as a bit bewildering:

The angels, that first inhabited this Region, where Thou art to bring forth a new Order of Beings, were great and powerful Spirits, highly endowed with the Riches and Powers of their Creator. Whilst they stood (as the Order of Creation requires) in Meekness and Resignation, under their Creator, nothing was impossible to them; there was no End of their glorious Powers throughout their whole Kingdom. Perpetual Scenes of Light, and Glory, and Beauty, were rising and changing through all the Height and Depth of their *glassy Sea*, merely at their Will and Pleasure. But finding what Wonders of Light and Glory they could perpetually bring forth; how all the *Powers* of Eternity, treasured up in their *glassy Sea*, unfolded themselves . . . they began to admire and adore themselves, and to fancy that there was *some Infinity of Power hidden* in themselves. . . .

Fired and intoxicated with this proud Imagination, they boldly resolved, with all their eternal Energy and Strength, to take their Kingdom, with all its Glories, to themselves, by eternally abjuring all Meekness and Submission to God.[59]

Intent upon exploring the implications of divine truth suggested to him by Jacob Boehme, Law constructs an embroidery of spiritual ideas which are intended to transport the mind and spirit into imaginative probabilities. Speaking of what takes place when man asserts free will for good or evil, he states:

. . . God sets before Man *Fire* and *Water*, *Life* and *Death* . . . these Things are not God . . . but they are that which is . . . called *Nature*. . . .

. . . In this twofold Life of the Creature, is Fire and Water, Life and Death . . . as its Will works with either of these Lives, so will it find either Fire or Water, Life or Death. If its Will turns from the Life of God, into the creaturely Life, then it enters into a *Sensibility* of that which is meant by Death and Fire, viz., a wrathful Misery. But if the Will keeps steadily given up to the Deity, then it lives in Possession of that *Life* and *Water*, which was its first, and will be its everlasting heavenly Joy and Happiness.[60]

From Law's point of view, knowing all of these details is not irrelevant to a life of devotion. He believes that before his readers can fully appreciate the true spirit of prayer they must first conduct their souls patiently over the intellectual path that leads to it. The first steps along that path must be taken, therefore, toward "right thinking." The will can operate efficiently only after the intellect has prepared the way.

As a rule, Law follows the literal account of Scripture as far as it goes in stating man's problems and answers; then he supplements that account with imaginative expositions of what he believes to be the plausible implications of biblical teaching. His mystical tendencies reveal themselves in such archetypal images as "light," "fire," and "darkness" to express the presence of good and evil in the play of forces in the divine nature. His speculative language is less like the philosophies of Spinoza and Hegel than that of the Theosophists who deduce by mystical insight the phenomenal world by doctrines of macrocosm and microcosm. These elaborations enable Law to avoid the oversimplifications of commonly accepted teachings and give him the opportunity to speculate upon spiritual probabilities.

In supplementing the scriptural account with plausible additions Law was no innovator. Both Milton and Dante, for example, far outdid him in their carefully knit embroidery of the biblical narrative, drawing at times upon mythology or history, or again explaining some great scriptural truth in the framework of the scientific theories of the day. And the general body of Christendom has not complained against these creative, if imaginative, systems of thought, since it had none better to offer. Yet few of Law's predecessors in devotional writing dwelt as much upon imaginative elaboration of Scripture as he.

VIII   *Devotional Tone*

If one is only partially convinced of the devotional character of *The Spirit of Prayer, The Spirit of Love* and *The Way to Divine Knowledge* after reviewing their dominant themes, he can hardly fail to discern the devotional tone that pervades these works. While here and there one notes a few departures from orthodox beliefs, these are minor when compared to the broader areas of agreement with the theological assumptions held by the general body of devotional writers: belief in an omnipotent, omniscient, holy God who ought to be worshiped; acceptance of man's accountability to God; viewing the Scriptures as containing the inerrant word of God. Law also followed reverently the standard teachings of the State Church concerning the sacraments and general rules for human conduct. His orthodoxy much more than his heterodoxy determines the tone of the later works.

One feels throughout the later works also that the same impulses that actuated the hearts of à Kempis, Fenelon, and St. Augustine were also throbbing for expression in William Law. While the system of thought with which he chose to express himself may appear inadequate, or at least awkward on occasion, one cannot help discerning what Colin Wilson speaks of as "the extraordinary serenity which breathes through the late works"[61] and that the spirit of devotion pulsates in perfect accord with that great company on earth who have professed a passion to lead men toward the glory ineffable.

Those who brand Law as a thorough-going mystic who preaches esoteric doctrine fail to note that the spiritual ideal that he holds up is within reach of everyone. He pours forth continually an anthem of praise and delight, as may be illustrated by the following quotation from *The Spirit of Prayer*:

O Holy Trinity, immense Ocean of Divine Love in which all Mankind live, and move, and have their Being! None are separated from Thee, none live out of thy Love, but all are embraced in the Arms of thy Mercy, all are Partakers of thy Divine Life, the Operation of thy Holy Spirit, as soon as their Heart is turned to Thee! Oh plain, and easy, and simple Way of Salvation, wanting no Subtleties of Art or Science, no borrowed Learning, no Refinements of Reason, but all done by the simple natural Motion of every Heart, that truly longs after God.[62]

The chief concern of every man, therefore, in a world where the enjoyment of the Divine is of paramount importance, is to cherish the spark of desire for God in the soul. This preoccupation with worship, or the fostering of divine life in the soul, contributes toward the devotional spirit which makes Law's later works rank as high in devotional attainment as anything else that he wrote and places them among other significant writings in the devotional tradition. The following prayer outlines the kind of life that the author would engender in the soul:

Oh Heavenly Father, infinite, fathomless Depth of never-ceasing Love, save me from myself, from the disorderly Workings of my fallen, long corrupted nature, and let my Eyes see, my Heart and Spirit feel and find, thy Salvation in Christ Jesus.[63]

As a devotional writer, Law sets for himself a very high objective and never falters until he achieves it; he would have men read significance and meaning into life. He is willing to discuss for a time the external helps which may advance man along his spiritual quest, but he does not stop until he has supplied a full-dressed account of the spiritual essence that underlies all phenomena. As Dante followed his philosopher-guide through the ten circles of hell and the seven cornices of purgatory but awaited the religious guidance of Beatrice and St. Bernard for conduct to the beatific vision, so Law proceeds at first over the road of conventional devotional rules and other prescribed courses of conduct, but does not rest until he beholds and worships at last at the inner shrine of Divine Reality.

The positive note discernible in most of Law's later writings persists to the end; the stamp of conviction never grows faint. The only salvation for man is "the life of God in the soul." There is only one way to attain to the life he has described, but that way is unmistakable to one who will heed the desire of the soul for higher things and uncompromisingly subscribe to a transformation of soul and new life in the Spirit. Happiness on earth can be known only in that way.

The devotional preoccupation remains uppermost in the late as in the early writings. As all the forerunners in devotional writing penned words of comfort, spiritual indoctrination, and exhortation to those of like faith, so Law faithfully sustains and feeds the fires of spiritual life which flickered in the lives of those of his own generation, and subsequently. Love becomes his terminus, for he believes this to be the goal of spiritual achievement. He says at the opening of the third dialogue in *The Spirit of Love*, "I can do nothing else but love; it is my whole Nature. I have no Taste for any Thing else. Can this matter be carried higher in Practice?"

With all his predilections for mysticism, Law constantly enjoins the believer to enact Christian precept into life. Hence, as one might expect, the hortatory manner prominent in *Christian Perfection* and *A Serious Call* persists in *The Spirit of Prayer, The Spirit of Love*, and *The Way to Divine Knowledge*:

... You have no questions to ask of any Body, no new Way that you need inquire after; no Oracle that you need to consult; for whilst you shut up yourself in Patience, Meekness, Humility, and Resignation to God, you are in the very Arms of Christ. . . .
... Stand therefore steadfastly in this *Will*, let nothing else enter into your Mind, have no other Contrivance, but everywhere, and in every Thing, to nourish and keep up *this State* of Heart, and then your House is built upon a Rock; you are safe from all Danger; the Light of Heaven, and the Love of God, will begin their Work in you, will bless and sanctify every Power of your fallen Soul. . . .[64]

When Law wrote *The Spirit of Love, The Spirit of Prayer* and *The Way to Divine Knowledge*, his sole purpose was to quicken the spiritual life of his readers. This he sought to do in two ways: first, by outlining a system of thought which he believed would, if received, place the believer in a constant spirit of prayer and love and set him on the way to divine knowledge; and second, by enjoining the worshiper to translate into the practical situations of life the moral precepts passed on to him. Admittedly, the emphasis fell upon the first of these, for Law inclined more and more to the belief that knowledge itself was virtue. He says in *The Spirit of Prayer*, "The measure of our Life is the Measure of our Knowledge; and as the Spirit of our Life works, so the Spirit of our Understanding conceives."[65] Of course, by knowledge Law means divine knowledge, which includes knowledge about God, as well as the personal knowledge of God. However, with all the involved discussions of death to self and new life in God found in the later works, Law still shows his concern for the implementation of Christian doctrine in practical living.

For Law, man's chief business in life is to live on a spiritual plane; hence, even his practical advice touches upon ways and means by which one may achieve greater piety. As he states in *The Way to Divine Knowledge*, "For Light is not only Life, but the Perfection, and highest State of it; and therefore nothing can bring forth Light, but that which can bring forth the Truth and Perfection of Life."[66]

The absence of specific references to current social and political issues and Law's aloofness from even the spiritual problems of the church have incurred for him charges of semi-asceticism and impracticality. Perhaps his esoteric discussions of Boehme's doctrines have lent some credence to these charges. And it can hardly be doubted that he alienated many readers through his determination to bring into the late writings so much discussion about the makeup of the universe and so many theoretical explanations of what was involved in man's fall and recovery. Yet, Law does not ignore entirely what he believes to be the major religious issues of his day. While he did not quibble with his fellow-churchmen over niceties of doctrine, particularly in the devotional works, he opposed strenuously the positions of those whom he believed to be true enemies of Christianity. In *The Way to Divine Knowledge* he indicts some of them specifically: "For every Man that cleaves to this World, that is in Love with it, and its earthly Enjoyments, is a disciple of *Epicurus*, and sticks in the same Mire of Atheism, as he did, whether he be a modern Deist, a Popish or Protestant Christian, an Arian, or an orthodox Teacher. For all these Distinctions are without any Difference, if this World has the Possession and Government of his Heart."[67]

Whether or not one accepts Law's pronouncements, one must at least concede that he was more sensitive to the larger theological problems of his day than to the bickerings among the church sects over petty matters of church government. For the most part, the devotional writings are remarkably free from contention or argument over metaphysical subtleties. Law states in the opening remarks of *The Spirit of Love*, "I have an utter Aversion to . . . Matters of Theological Debate . . . as . . . Contentions merely of a Worldly Nature. . . . I consider . . . only . . . Motives and Occasions of edifying both you and myself with the Truth, the Power, and Divine Blessedness of the *Spirit* of *Love*."[68]

In all, he did not ask his readers to forsake the responsibilities of the world in which they lived—either political or social. Rather, he implied that the first duty of those involved in public affairs was correct alignment of religious perspectives. Law's emphasis, therefore, is similar to such devotional predecessors as St. Augustine, Joseph Hall, and Lancelot Andrewes, who did not ignore the primary matters of faith, but who at the same time conceived that faith in a spirit of practical application to everyday life.

CHAPTER 5

Law's Enduring Achievement

I Devotional Prose Style

IN his study of the development of English prose, George Krapp
contends that devotional prose in general may claim some
contribution to the artistic development of the English language from
the colloquial, blunt Anglo-Saxon idiom to the later, more dignified
manner of expression which appealed more directly to the mind and
to the heart.[1] The change from the earliest verse to prose was only
gradual and came about under the hard necessity of instructing
people about the many complications of ordinary life. Krapp
includes among the early prose writers who distinguished themselves
in the artistic expression of words of instruction and edification some
of the names we have encountered in this study: Richard Rolle,
Lancelot Andrewes, compilers of the Bible and Prayer Books, and
such a sermonizer as Henry Smith.

Devotionalist Helen McHugh characterizes the religious prose of
the medieval period as still owing a debt to the Latin writers, but
showing through the use of figures of speech and images drawn from
everyday life a homeliness, humor, and charm not to be found in the
more formal, conventional imagery of the Latin originals.[2] Although
written by educated men, the newer prose was much closer to the
speech of the people. Even where echoes of patristic imagery occur,
the similes and metaphors have much more picturesqueness and
charm than earlier.

Helen White describes the devotional prose of the sixteenth and
seventeenth centuries as "straightforward, direct, incisive"—much in
keeping with other literatures which were written in the current of the
times.[3] More symbolic and figurative than in the preceding centuries,
this prose also became more sensuous than hitherto in an effort to
bring religious truth home not only to the intellect, but to the
imagination and feeling.

One notices underneath the vitality and unremitting earnestness of these writers of devotional prose a keen sensitivity to style. With all of their emphasis upon practicing the presence of God, inquiring into the inner life, and orienting practical interests in the light of eternal truth, they sought to employ the apt phrases and figures of speech that would serve as appropriate clothing for their lofty and noble thoughts.

One cannot read the works of William Law without being impressed that he, too, was sensitive to technique as well as content. Many students of Law have concurred in their praise of his prose style. Caroline Spurgeon spoke of Law as "among the greatest of English prose writers." Of his later writings she said, "They have a tolerance, a tender charm, an imaginative quality . . . rarely found in the early work," while their subject matter has "a strength and beauty which Plotinus has rarely surpassed."[4] Ralph Inge commends his mastery of "a striking and attractive English style."[5] Hopkinson and Gibbon also paid him extravagant compliments as a prose stylist; ". . . His precepts are rigid," wrote Gibbon, "but they are founded on the Gospel; his satire is sharp, but it is drawn from the knowledge of human life, and many of his portraits are not unworthy of the pen of La Bruyere."[6]

In a real sense, with Law, as with many other devotionalists, the style is the man; his manner of life and texture of thought and expression can hardly be separated. Strikingly evident are his simplicity, clarity, and vividness. Typical of the eighteenth-century religious mind who eschewed the pedantry of the seventeenth-century divine, Law achieves a pungency and forcefulness through a lucid and direct manner, especially in his early works. Colin Wilson spoke of it as "clear, hard-hitting prose," much in common with Blaise Pascal.[7] The simple, clear, transparent language, which he casts in short sentences and paragraphs, creates a certain charm and beauty. Law's aim is to be first explicit, then persuasive.

Law's logical power stands alongside his clarity of expression. His was a closely logical habit of mind which acted upon all that he experienced emotionally and spiritually. The result was that he appealed to the intellect of his readers while challenging them to fervency in religion. His habitual writing formula is to lay down a general principle and then pursue it to a logical conclusion. He admits no evasion in plying the lukewarm Christian, while refraining from a contentious or argumentative spirit.[8] Caroline Spurgeon also speaks of his keen flashes of wit and "grim satire" and adds:

On this side his was a true eighteenth-century mind, logical, sane, practical, with . . . a touch of whimsey. . . . When he was still a young man, the logical and satirical side was strongest; in late years, this was much tempered by emotion and tenderness.[9]

Although Law's logical power is outstanding in his controversial writings, it is equally prominent in the devotional treatises, where he urges the professing Christian toward greater heights in pious living.

One of Law's favorite devices for argument is the *reductio ad absurdum*, which is well illustrated in the story of the pond, where he shows the absurdity of a man living in continual thirst who owns a large pond, but who wastes time and strength to replenish the water without slaking his own thirst and at last drowns in the pond:

Again, if you should see a man that had a large *pond* of *water*, yet living in *continual thirst*, not suffering himself to drink *half a draught*, for fear of lessening the pond; if you should see him wasting his time and strength, in fetching more water to his pond, always *thirsty*, yet always carrying a *bucket* of water in his hand, watching early and late to catch the *drops* of rain, gaping after every cloud, and running greedily into every *mire* and *mud* in hopes of water, and always studying how to make every *ditch* empty itself into his *pond*. If you should see him grow *grey* and *old* in these anxious labours, and at last end a *careful, thirsty* life, by falling into his own *pond*, would you not say, that such a one was not only the author of all his own disquiets, but was foolish enough to be reckoned amongst *idiots* and *madmen*? But yet foolish and absurd as this character is, it does not represent half the follies, and absurd disquiets of the *covetous man*.[10]

The logical structure may be seen even in the general architecture of the sentences. Characteristically he will place "if . . . then" clauses in sequence:

If therefore these are always alive in us, always driving, or governing our Lives, if we can have no Holiness or Goodness, but as this Life of Thought, Will, and Affection, works in us, if we are all called to this inward Holiness and Goodness, then a *perpetual, always existing Operation of the Spirit of God within us*, is absolutely necessary. . . .

Now if our Thoughts, Wills, and Affections, need only be now and then holy and good, then, indeed, the moving and breathing Spirit of God need only now and then govern us. But if our Thoughts and Affections are to be always holy and good, then the holy and good Spirit of God is to be always operating, as a Principle of Life within us.[11]

Sometimes Law will begin a series of long paragraphs with an "if" and move toward a logical conclusion at the close of each paragraph.[12]

When Henri Talon refers to *Christian Perfection* and *A Serious Call* as "studies in the art of persuasion," he underlines the hortatory manner which one finds everywhere in these treatises. As illustration, the final chapter of *Christian Perfection,* entitled "An Exhortation to Christian Perfection," portrays Law's hope and expectation that the ideal he has been advocating will be translated into practical living. After summarizing the reasonableness and urgency of his former arguments, he extols the happiness of a life of devotion in this world: "I believe there are very few Christians who have it not in their Heads at least to be some Time or other Holy and Virtuous and readily own that He is the happy Man that dies truly Humble, Holy, and Heavenly-Minded."[13] The exhortation to seek perfection follows:

If you would now devote yourself to Perfection, perhaps you must part with some Friends, you must displease some Relations, you must lay aside some Designs, you must refrain from some Pleasures, you must alter your Life, nay, perhaps you must expose yourself to the Hatred of your Friends, to the Jest and Ridicule of *Wits*, and to the Scorn and Derision of worldly men.[14]

For sentence variation Law may construct a whole paragraph, using a series of parallel sentences which have infinitive phrases for subjects.[15] Again, he may build a paragraph upon a succession of rhetorical questions.[16] Typical also is his use of the apostrophe, a practice frequently followed in the eighteenth century.[17] Or he may repeat key words in successive sentences for cumulative effect; more frequently, he will present a series of parallel clauses. This latter technique, which repeats similar sentence elements in succession, is well adapted to his characteristic manner of exploring the many sides of a topic.

Another sentence pattern common to his writings is the "as . . . so" construction, which he uses in presenting his analogies:

For as our souls, in a great measure, depend upon our bodies, and as we have great power over our bodies, as we can commend our outward actions, and oblige ourselves to such habits of life, as naturally produce habits in the soul, as we can mortify our bodies, and remove ourselves, from objects that inflame our passions, so we have a great power over the *inward* state of our souls. Again, as we are masters of our outward actions, as we can force ourselves to outward acts of reading, praying, singing, and the like, and as all these bodily actions have an effect upon the soul, as they naturally tend to form such and such tempers in our hearts; so by being masters of these outward, bodily actions, we have great power over the inward state of the heart.[18]

Law's determination to be understood prompted him to use figures of speech that could be grasped by the average layman. Frequently his analogies are of the most elementary and universal kind; for instance, he may speak of the similitude of "a grain of wheat," "air," "light," "ocean," "husk," and "pearl of eternity." The analogies at times are even homely:

But if, with sound and good Legs, you would not stir one Step, till you had got *Crutches* to hop with, surely a Man might show you the Folly of not walking with your own Legs, without being thought a declared Enemy to Crutches, or the Makers of them. Now a *Manual* is not so good an Help, as Crutches, and yet you see Crutches are only proper, when our Legs cannot do their Office.[19]

In another place Law says, "Now can anyone say, that the strictest rules of such a religion as this, debar us of any of the comforts of life? Might it not as justly be said of those rules, which only hindered a man from *choking* himself with *gravel*?"[20]

The later works frequently employ figures appropriate to the mystical experience, with images from St. John's Apocalypse, such as "fire," "light," "darkness," and "glassy sea." Passages of unusual beauty result from his frequent attempts to employ figures that match his depth of thought and insight:

The Sea neither is, nor can be moved and tossed by any other Wind, than that which has its Birth, and Life, and Strength, in and from the Sea itself, as its *own Wind*. The Sun in the Firmament gives Growth to every Thing that grows in the Earth, and Life to every Thing that lives upon it. . . .

The *stinking Gum* gives nothing to the Soul, nor brings any Thing into Sensibility, but that which was before in the Soul, it has only a Fitness to awaken. . . .

Again, the greatest Artist in *Music* can add *no Sound* to his Instrument, nor make it give forth any other Melody, but that which lies *silently hidden in it*, as its own inward State.[21]

Law may not have striven meticulously to achieve a magic of words, but he was sensitive to the literary devices of other craftsmen in an age distinguished for its literary prose. That he was not oblivious to style is indicated as he spoke of his dislike of "loose and declamatory writings."[22] Particularly in his later works, his balance of phrase, cadence, parallel structure, and elaborate sentences helped to earn for him a literary prose reputation.

Law has been accused of occasional stiffness and lack of music in his early prose, as in the following passage:

Now the reason of common swearing is this, it is because men have not so much as the *intention to please God in all their actions*. For let a man but have so much piety as to *intend to please God in all the actions of his life, as the happiest and best thing in the world*, and then he will never swear more. It will be as impossible for him to swear, whilst he feels *this intention* within himself, as it is impossible for a man who intends to please his Prince, to go up and abuse him to his face.[23]

No doubt the solemn, sonorous prose of the King James Bible exerted an influence upon Law's language. But, as literary critic Henri Talon notes, "If lyricism is both music and the surge of deepest feelings, then Law is often lyrical." And as his "mind and thoughts traveled to heaven," he employs naturally a rhythmic and melodious style, replete with appropriate images.

One of the outstanding literary innovations that Law brings to his early devotional treatises to embellish his precepts of devotion is his use of imaginary prose characters. The literary genre known as the "character" sets forth concrete descriptions of representative human or ethical types and owes its origin to Theophrastus of the fourth century B.C.[24] Although the thirty characters of Theophrastus which have come down to us have no immediate imitators, Isaac Casaubon's translation of Theophrastus's characters into Latin in 1592 and 1599 stimulated a revival of the form. The first original English production was Joseph Hall's *Characters of Vertues and Vices* in 1608; others of the same century who helped to perfect the type were Sir Thomas Overbury and John Earle. Addison, Steele, and other periodical essayists used the character to delineate human types in the eighteenth century.

Most of the seventeenth-century character writers worked according to a precise pattern, consisting usually of an opening generalization, central development, and conclusion. Although Law undoubtedly owes a debt to his forerunners in character writing, he did not follow completely their patterns or forms. His usual procedure is to cite a character as illustration of a general truth he has been advocating. Then he lists the moral characteristics and patterns of conduct that typify the one he is portraying. Law's manner of handling the character to depict moral types may be variously illustrated. For example, there is Patronus, who loves the beauty of buildings:

Patronus is fond of a Clergyman who understands *Music, Painting, Statuary,* and *Architecture.* He is an Enemy to the *Dissenters,* and loves the *Church of England* because of the *Stateliness* and *Beauty* of its Buildings; he never comes to the *Sacrament,* but will go forty Miles to see a fine *Altarpiece.*[25]

Another illustration of one who lets a wrong temper interfere with the impressions of true religion is Lycia, an easy-going, gay person:

Lycia has no wicked or irreligious Temper, and she might be pious, but that she is too *easy, gay,* and *cheerful,* to admit of Care of any Kind. She can no more *repent,* than she can be *out of Temper,* and must be the same *sparkling, cheerful* Creature in the *Church,* as in the *Playhouse.*[26]

One sees at once that Law's purpose is to depict a human type more than to describe literally a living person. In fact, one feels that most of the time Law uses the names of his characters merely as pegs on which to hang his moralizations.

Leslie Stephen states that "the predominantly logical character of Law may be seen in his sketches."[27] Hopkinson is somewhat lavish in his assessment, "His cameo-like delineations of various human types will never be forgotten as long as English literature survives; they are like the homely parables of Jesus; they do more than enforce his teaching—they enshrine it. They are the hypodermic needles of truth."[28] However, he adds somewhat more realistically, ". . . in spite of all that has been said about William Law's character sketches . . . they are perfect: too good or too bad, too wise or too silly to be the kind of human beings we meet in modern daily life."

Even though one may feel that Law's portraits are not sharp enough and frequently not long enough to constitute a recognizable human type, they are a welcome relief from the straightforward, expository manner in which he habitually writes. They demonstrate his good stock of abstract words and illustrate his imaginative approach to devotional literature by his employing a device which gave greater life and immediacy to the precepts of devotion he was enjoining.

The early eighteenth century, with its predilection for satire, which saw Pope writing his Epistles, Swift leveling his criticisms against English life, and Addison deriding the foibles and eccentricities of persons who deviated from the norms in English society, was a suitable setting for the satirical manner which one discerns in Law's character portraits and elsewhere. Although one cannot trace specific influences upon him to any of the prominent writers of satire who flourished in that period, Law is similar to his contemporary, Alexander Pope, in at least one outstanding respect. Just as Pope was adept at flailing his adversary at his precise point of basic weakness, so Law attacked what he believed to be the most vulnerable and irrefutable point in the position of the professing Christian.

A variation of Law's early use of the "character" occurs in the later works where he turns to dialogues in the manner of Plato. In Part Two of *The Spirit of Prayer* the subject for discussion was ways of leading the soul "out of the vanity of time into the riches of eternity." The names of the participants suggest their respective points of view: Academicus, Rusticus, Theophilus, and Humanus. The conversations are often stilted and unnatural, but the differing points of view are argued cogently, and through a synthesis of views expressed Law drives home the key points with which he seeks to deepen and enrich spiritual outlook. As Philo said to Academicus concerning the devotional intent of the conversations, "All this . . . is said on your Account that, you may not lose the Benefit of this Spark of the Divine Life that is kindled in your Soul, but may conform yourself suitably to so great a Gift of God."[29]

Platonic dialogue, while something of an innovation in devotional literature, was not uncommon in other types of prose in the seventeenth and eighteenth centuries. One can readily recall the polite conversations in Dryden's *Essay of Dramatic Poesy* and Walton's *Compleat Angler* as illustrations of the technique. Law adapts the leisurely, exploratory technique of the Platonic dialogue in his elaborations of diverse points of view upon religion. The following conversational exchange is typical of his manner:

Rusticus. Pray, Gentlemen, let an unlearned Man speak a Word here. Suppose, *Academicus*, you had a longing earnest Desire, to be governed by a Spirit of *Plainness* and *Sincerity* in your whole Conversation. Would this put you upon asking for *Art*, and *Rules*, and *Methods*, or consulting some learned Man, or Book, to direct you, and keep you from Delusion? . . .

Academicus. I do not know how to understand what *Rusticus* has said. For do not all good Christians daily pray for the Spirit of God? Yet how few are led by it? Pray, *Theophilus*, do you speak here.

Theophilus. . . . But you are to observe, that *Rusticus* spoke of the *Spirit of Prayer*, which is the Heart's own Prayer, and which has all the Strength of Heart in it. And this is the Prayer that must be affirmed to be *always* effectual; it never returns empty; it eats and drinks that, after which it hungers and thirsts; and nothing can possibly hinder it from having that, which it prays for. . . .[30]

The flow of Law's writings is not always regular. As Robert Burton said of his own style in his *Anatomy of Melancholy*, it is ". . . as a river . . . sometimes precipitate and swift, then dull and slow, now direct, then *per ambages*, now deep, then shallow. . . ." Speaking of the alternating tempos of Law's works, Talon comments that Law proceeds as "a man in quest of the truth who proceeds by leaps and bounds and finds things as he goes."[31] However, his diction is usually majestic and rolls along with the strong surge of a mind that is confident of its message.

II *Law's Influence: General Acclaim*

No attempt is made here to take a full measure of Law's perennial influence, but it may be useful at least to look at the reactions to his works by numerous responsible people to indicate somewhat his popularity and then to examine in more detail the extent of his devotional influence upon two prominent English figures, Samuel Johnson and John Wesley.

A great deal has already been said in this study about the popularity and influence of the *Serious Call*. If, as some assert, the works of Law were read in his day by only a "coterie of disciples," it becomes difficult to explain the impact of this work upon so many diverse minds and its passing through numerous editions.[32] As historian John Millar points out:

Addressed to the professing Christian, and not to the professing sceptic, it plies him with every possible incentive to accommodate his conduct to his creed; and its effect upon contemporary religious thought can hardly be exaggerated. Wilberforce's *Practical View* is the only book . . . which can vie with it in popularity and influence.[33]

Whatever fascination the *Serious Call* may have held for the reading public, chief interest focused upon its devotional characteristics.

The list of those who have felt a "reverential awe" for the book grows long and impressive. John Keble pays it tribute. Dr. Newman, after speaking of what he owed to Calvinistic teaching, adds, "This main catholic warfare between the 'City of God' and the powers of darkness was also deeply impressed upon my mind by a work of a character very opposite to Calvinism, Law's *Serious Call*."[34] James A. Froude is reported to have kept Law on his table more than any other. One nineteenth-century reviewer praised its devotional power thus:

You may read the book and think first that it is amusing, then that it is clever, then that it is penetrating in its sagacity, then that it is an excellent description of such and such an aspect of worldliness; but at last, without a moment's warning, the book finds you yourself, and your attention is riveted by a piercing sentence which strikes into your very soul.[35]

One popular eighteenth-century book recommended that ministerial candidates ought to read Cicero, Xenophon, Plutarch, Seneca, Epictetus, Marcus Aurelius, Juvenal, and of Christian moralists, More's *Ethics*, Taylor's *Holy Living* and *Holy Dying*, and especially Law's *Serious Call*.[36]

Augustine Birrell in his *Res Judicatae* describes William Law as "the inimitable author of the *Serious Call*." Speaking of Gibbon's achievement of learning and industry in *The Decline and Fall* he said, ". . . it is more lasting than marble, yet in sundry moods it seems but a poor and barren thing by the side of a book which, like the *Serious Call*, has proved its power to pierce the heart and tame the will."[37] Charles Williams comments, "Law wrote in . . . retirement a few books which . . . form perhaps one of the best statements of the pure Christian religion that have ever been issued."[38] Rufus Jones pays tribute to Law as a "saint" and "prophet" of the soul. He speaks of those who have operated in and through certain men of history, shaping and altering the course of human events, and singles out Law from his century as one who "lifted up the Christian way of life in an age of doubt and skepticism and denial" and who gave such a vivid and powerful interpretation of the rightly fashioned life that it stood out "as the most vital interpretation of his century."[39] Jones thinks of a saint as a rare specimen who has refined his soul and who, through entering into close contact with the life of God, has discovered a "new level of life and power." Speaking upon the same subject, William James says that placed alongside them (saints) "the strong men of this world . . . [are] seen as dry sticks, as hard and crude as blocks of stones or brickbats."[40] Both Jones and James were referring particularly to *A Serious Call*. Historian Edward Gibbon said, "In our family William Law left the reputation of a worthy and pious man who believed all that he professed and practiced all that he enjoined."

One clergyman writes as follows of his attempt to promote piety among his parishioners:

. . . I preached amongst them incessantly, and yet, after all, was convinced my work had been as fruitless as casting pearls before swine; the drunkard continued his nocturnal practices, and the voice of the swearer was still heard in our streets. However, I was determined to leave no means untried for bringing this profane and obdurate people to a sense of their duty: accordingly, I purchased many religious books and distributed them . . . ; but, alas! I could perceive no visible effects. . . . About this time I happened to peruse a treatise of Mr. Law's entitled, *A Serious Call to a Devout and Holy Life*, with which I was so charmed and greatly edified, that I resolved my flock should partake of the same spiritual food. I, therefore, gave to each person in my parish one of those useful books . . . and I had the satisfaction of beholding my people reclaimed from a life of folly and impiety to a life of holiness and devotion.[41]

Francis Okeley, an educated university man, a translator of German mystical writings, and evangelical preacher, wrote the following excerpt in one of his letters after visiting Law:

Happy should I esteem myself, if out of the mouth or pen of two or three witnesses, the good opinion of the general utility of Mr. Law's writings could be so far established, that ministers and people of every denomination might be inclined seriously to read, and truly to perform the sound practice of his words. Although we are to call no man "Master" on earth, because there is only one that is perfect and infallible, yet I can with truth aver, that I have reason to believe the Lord hath spoken and doth yet speak to this age by him.[42]

Three comparatively recent studies have paid tribute to *A Serious Call* as making a contribution to the general body of religious thought. The first of these by John MacNeill places the work with those of Luther, Calvin, Hooker, Bunyan, and the Wesleys as a book which expresses the "basic elements of the Christian tradition," and ranks it with the popular seventeenth-century guides to the devout life.[43] A study by Hugh Martin also lists some books which he believes have survived the test of time as books that "are concerned with God's intimate dealings with the human soul."[44] He insists that man must know how to reconstruct his own life before he can help rebuild society, and that Law qualifies admirably for giving the kind of help needed. He also praises Law for not withdrawing from life into idle meditation, as many mystics have done, but for invading life "armed with new creative powers." Also, Colin Wilson includes Law in his general treatment of those of history who have dared to strike out as rebels against mediocrity and spiritual apathy. He praises Law's "clear-cut, hard-hitting prose" which portrays the attitude of a man who hungers for reality and purpose in living.[45] C. S. Lewis writes of *A Serious Call* ". . . about prides, superiorities, and affronts there is no better book. [There] you'll find all of us pierced like butterflies on cards."[46]

An illustration of the far-reaching effect that the *Serious Call* has produced upon twentieth-century minds was seen when a group of businessmen from a prominent church in a large mid-western American city, after choosing quite by accident Law's *Serious Call* as a manual of devotion for their periodic noonday gatherings, decided to compile an abridgment of the work for the benefit of other modern readers. Their enthusiasm for Law may be seen in one of their testimonials:

> . . . the idea that ultimately gave rise to this book has also transformed our church. The prayer cell that produced this abridgment has included wholesale grocers, factory workers, physicians, lawyers, and salesmen. . . . As the weeks passed into months and as our group grew larger, we came to feel that Law was one of our number. He seemed to speak directly to us! For anyone to suggest . . . that we change books would be tantamount to betraying a faithful friend.[47]

Law's effectiveness is acknowledged naturally by persons of intense personal piety, but G. G. Perry writes that even "the gay men of the world"—frequenters of coffeehouses and clubs were impressed by this spokesman of religion.[48] An interesting and significant illustration of the effect produced by Law upon a mind not naturally disposed toward religion was the case of John Byrom, who tells us how he was affected and who left a minute record of Law's influence upon several of his contemporaries.[49]

Most of Law's perennial popularity has been based upon his early writings, with *A Serious Call* and *Christian Perfection* holding the spotlight. *The Spirit of Love, The Spirit of Prayer*, and *The Way to Divine Knowledge*, although treating the same themes and vibrating with the same devotional fervor, did not at first capture the same interest for readers largely because of their association with mysticism. As a result, these works fell out of print and into almost total eclipse. Yet the few patient scholars who have read sympathetically the later writings have discovered not only that Law manifests there an underlying unity of thought and warmth of devotion, but that, as Christopher Walton, W. R. Inge, Alexander Whyte, and others contend, the late works represent the more brilliant flame of his genius. An early reviewer reminds us: "It is impossible to enter into the spirit of any of his writings . . . earlier or later . . . without perceiving both a mental and spiritual stimulus."[50]

The most recent attempt to rescue these later works from oblivion has been that of Stephen Hobhouse who gathered excerpts from each of them and put them together in one volume in the hope that modern readers might catch a glimpse of their beauty and sense the impact of their devotional appeal. Future readers may discover that their value as literature of devotion has been underestimated and accord them a reappraisal. Hitherto, however, Law's late writings have suffered neglect.

III *Devotional Influence on Samuel Johnson and John Wesley*

That Law's perennial influence is unmistakable may be seen in the general tributes paid to him. A closer look at the effect Law's thought produced upon two contemporaries will illustrate more fully the nature and extent of that influence.

A review of the principal studies of Law's thought indicates that Samuel Johnson was deeply affected by the former's devotional precepts. Stuart Brown sees Law's influence at work when Johnson makes his rules for self-improvement.[51] Walter Jackson Bate speaks of *A Serious Call* as "a moving devotional work—the finest of its kind written during the century";[52] he also pays tribute to it as the inspiration for Johnson's moral writings—particularly in its insisting upon the futility of seeking human happiness in anything outside of the hope for eternity.[53] Katherine Balderston attempts to assess the true effect of Law upon his eminent contemporary in the light of Johnson's well-known statement that Law was "quite an overmatch" for him.[54] Johnson wrote to Boswell that he had fallen into "inattention" and "indifference" about religion until "[I] took up

Law's *Serious Call to a [Devout and] Holy Life* expecting to find it a dull book (as such books generally are), and perhaps to laugh at it. But I found Law quite an overmatch for me; and this was the first occasion of my thinking in earnest of religion after I became aware of rational inquiry."[55] Balderston points out that when Johnson read Law for the first time, he was only nineteen years old and a student at Oxford University where he was "a sort of lax talker." Since he had probably read the whole body of Christian literature from the Church Fathers down to his own day, he may have been largely unconscious of his debt to Law. The two men had broad areas of agreement in their ideas, although they were opposite in temper, range of interests, and natural endowment.

It is quite possible that Law's dogmatic "either or" alternatives, his rigid perfectionism, and his view of the nature of man may have turned Johnson toward a more realistic and balanced view in his later life. Nevertheless, Johnson never alters his regard for the Non-juror which he expressed earlier. It is also significant that in his *Dictionary*, published in 1755, he quotes *Christian Perfection* under "devotion" and, as noted earlier, makes frequent references throughout to *A Serious Call*. Although James Clifford associates the depression of Samuel Johnson with the reading of *A Serious Call*, he acknowledges indirectly the power of Law's devotional injuctions upon one of the eighteenth century's greatest minds.[56]

It is true that Johnson was impatient with the Behmenistic language of the later devotional works, but from his many kind tributes to Law and the parallels that exist between the two men in their views of moral responsibility, disciplines of the Christian tradition, and devotional habits, one may conclude safely that Law's abiding influence lay in his recommendations for spiritual betterment. In fact, as Katherine Balderston implies, Johnson's own composition of "Meditations and Devotional Exercises" may owe its inspiration to Law.[57]

The profound impact made by Law upon John Wesley is even more impressive. It is not possible here to analyze all of the connections between the two men; recent studies by J. B. Green and Eric Baker have traced in some detail the more important relationships.[58] However, Law's influence upon Wesley is striking, not only because of the great impetus which the latter gave to Evangelicalism in general and Methodism in particular, but because the devotional impact of Law's message accounts for far more of the influence than do theological considerations. Even when Wesley turned from Law for his mysticism, he could not resist long the power of his devotional attraction.

Touching upon this point, Green notes that in spite of Wesley's opposition to mysticism, the latter's emphasis upon the doctrine of Assurance drove him much nearer to Law's subjective emphasis than he might admit. Wesley wanted to be biblically authoritative, yet he, too, would corroborate that authority by an authentic interpretation from the inward witness of the Spirit. And, as Green says, "Mystical appreciation and evangelical faith . . . are in closest company."[59] Baker also claims that Law's treatises kindled in Wesley a passion for an ethical ideal that "remained unimpaired by his rejection of the mystical system."[60]

A study of Wesley's *Journal* and the correspondence that passed between the two men discloses that Law's abiding influence lay in his devotional injunctions. Whether the Methodist leader talked to Law personally, or read his treatises, it was invariably Law's devotional fervor that challenged him to greater spiritual achievement. When Wesley temporarily turned from Law as an unsatisfactory religious guide, his reason was a theological one. But he never accused Law of any diminution of devotional intensity, and evidence supports the view that late in Wesley's career he again spoke highly of the power of Law's writings as a shaping, molding influence, and continued to recommend them as edifying reading for young Christians.

Wesley visited Law at Putney several times between 1732 and 1735 and a close relationship developed between the two men. On one occasion Law gave Wesley a copy of *Theologia Germanica*.[61] This is the period in which Law became a kind of "oracle" to Wesley. The latter candidly admits that he tried to regulate his life after the manner of *A Serious Call*. Anxious about a student, he wrote a letter to Law on June 26, 1734, which evidences the esteem in which he holds his associate:

I must earnestly beg your immediate advice in a case of the greatest importance. About two years ago, I was entrusted with a young gentleman of good sense, an even generous temper, and pretty good learning. Religion he had heard little of. . . . I therefore beseech you, sir, by the mercies of God, that you will not be slack, according to the ability He shall give, to advise and pray for him.[62]

The following excerpts from the *Journal* in 1735 indicate the continued influence of the Non-Juror upon Wesley's thought:

Fri. 21 Nov., 1735. [I visited Mrs. Lawley] recovering from a dangerous illness . . . I thought it concerned her to be first instructed in the nature of Christianity, and accordingly fixed an hour a day to read with her in Mr. Law's treatise on Christian Perfection . . .

Mon. 24 Nov., 1735. . . . . The books read privately or publicly during these days are Wall *On Baptism, Nicodemus*, Law's *Christian Perfection*, Johnson's *Unbloody Sacrifice*, and the *Life of Gregory Lopez*.[63]

In a journal entry for May, 1738, Wesley, referring to the time prior to his appointment in 1726 as Fellow of Lincoln College, says:

. . . But meeting now with Mr. Law's *Christian Perfection* and *Serious Call*, although I was much offended at many parts of both, yet they convinced me more than ever of the exceeding height and breadth and depth of the law of God. The light flowed in so mightily upon my soul, that everything appeared in a new view. . . .[64]

There is little doubt that John Wesley's awakening owed a debt to the spiritual ideal extolled by Law. The unrest fostered in his spirit moved him to seek earnestly and persistently for ways to alleviate it. Of course, Law was not the only influence which Wesley felt. But, as Curnock avers, "for his definite reawakening . . . Wesley was indebted largely to the teaching of certain devotional books."[65] Listed are Thomas à Kempis's *Imitation of Christ*, or *Christian Pattern*; Bishop Jeremy Taylor's *Holy Living* and *Holy Dying*; William Law's *Christian Perfection*.

Specifically, in a letter from London, dated May 14, 1738, Wesley writes of his debt to Law, although a rupture between the two was imminent:

For two years . . . I have been preaching after the model of your two practical treatises, and all that heard have allowed that the law is great, wonderful, and holy. But no sooner did they attempt to fulfill it but they found that it is too high for man, and that by doing "the works of the law" shall no flesh be justified.[66]

Wesley then chides Law for his shortcomings and exhorts him, "Once more, sir, let me beg you to consider whether your extreme roughness, and morose and sour behavior, at least on many occasions, can possibly be the fruit of a living faith in Christ. If not, may the God of peace and love fill up what is yet wanting in you."[67] Wesley is wondering why Law has not emphasized faith as the sole means of salvation.

This outburst by Wesley, completely out of harmony with his previous attitude, must be interpreted in the light of the intellectual and spiritual conflict through which Wesley was passing. It is an over-simplification to say that Wesley fell out with Law simply because the latter became identified with the mystics. Actually, Wesley was searching for inner peace and was already following a high practical Christian standard. He saw in Law's works directives for a holy life that accelerated his quest for perfect obedience. But as he endeavored to measure up to the high standards, and as he enjoined others to follow suit, he came to believe that the mainspring of Law's emphasis was weak. Of course, the breach between the two broadened as Jacob Boehme's doctrines became discernible in Law. But the first murmur of dissent by Wesley began in the area of devotional negativism in which Law was charged with holding up an unattainable ideal. Wesley did not persist long in this objection, however, as subsequent evidence reveals.

To the above letter Law replied by pointing out a strange incon-sistency in Wesley's charges. He referred to their previous discussion of à Kempis and reminded Wesley that as earlier he had recom-mended à Kempis's devotional works to Wesley and had felt that basically no difference existed between them, à Kempis seemed to serve very well as a meeting ground on points of doctrine. Yet Wesley now said that Law was ignorant of some of these same doctrines. The verbal exchange, however, only heightened further misunderstand-ing. Wesley was engaged at the time in translating à Kempis and felt that Law was criticizing his qualifications for making such a translation, whereas Law had meant only to prove that the other's charges against him were unfounded, for the two men's mutual agreement on the teachings of à Kempis ought to indicate their general unanimity.

Wesley's "Aldersgate experience" of May 24, 1738, together with Law's further detour into the bypaths of mysticism, served to widen the breach between them.[68] Thereafter the men pursued separate paths, never visited each other again, and only occasionally made mention of the other. Several entries in the *Journal* and some of the letters cast light upon this phase of their relationship. A few of them are offered here:

Tues. 23 Oct., 1739. In riding to Bradford I read over Mr. Law's book on the

New Birth: philosophical, speculative, precarious, Behmenish, void and vain. . . .[69]

Curnock also includes the remarks of Charles Wesley made about the same time: "I read part of Mr. Law on Regeneration to our society. How promising the beginning! How lame the conclusion." John Wesley in the *Journal*, 27 July, 1749, praises some things about *The Spirit of Prayer* but denounces Law's treatment of the point of God's never being angry.

Wesley began a long, open letter to Law December 15, 1755, which was designed to counteract the evil done by Law's *Spirit of Love* and *Spirit of Prayer*. The letter was sent January 6, 1756. In it Wesley insists that the inspired Scriptures alone avail. He says Law "would have a philosophical religion, but there can be no such thing."[70] Speaking of the two works, Wesley says, "The whole of it [*Spirit of Love* and *Spirit of Prayer*] is utterly superfluous . . . [;] the hypothesis has a dangerous tendency by leading to a knowledge that puffeth up. . . . It is contrary to Scripture, to reason, and to itself."[71] He doubts the logical basis of Law's theory of creation and of his novel explanation of Adam's state and his subsequent fall, and he is particularly reluctant to accept Law's explanation of God's omnipotence and justice and his account of the new birth. Wesley closes the long letter thus:

O that your latter works may be more and greater than your first! Surely they would if you could ever be persuaded to study instead of the writings of Tauler and Behmen, those of St. Paul, James, Peter, and John . . . to renounce, despise, abhor all the high-flown bombast, all the intelligent jargon of the Mystics and come back to the plain religion of the Bible.[72]

To this letter Law did not reply directly, but commented briefly in a letter to a friend in 1756: "I was once a kind of Oracle with Mr. Wesley. I never suspected anything bad of him, or even discovered any kind or degree of falseness or hypocrisy in him. But during all the time of his intimacy with me, I judged him to be much more under the power of his own spirit. . . . It was owing to his unwillingness or unability to give up his own spirit that he was forced into that false and rash censure which he published in print against the mystics."[73] Again, in a letter dated September 7 of the same year he said that

To answer Mr. Wesley's letter is quite needless. [It] . . . is such a juvenile composition of emptiness and pertness as is below the character of any man who had been serious in religion for half a month.[74]

That Wesley defected from Law for a time is indisputable. He had some doctrinal reservations about Law and feared the misleading effect his mystical teachings might have. However, as time passed, Wesley saw the whole matter in perspective and became convinced that their common belief was more striking than their doctrinal differences. One notes a modification of Wesley's previous censorious attitude to the point that he admitted late in life the perennial benefit that may accrue to the believer who reads Law's works. In 1768 Wesley brought out as a part of his "Christian Library" two volumes of extracts from Law's later works (i.e., those published after *A Serious Call*). His inclusion of selections from *The Spirit of Prayer* and the last work, *Address to the Clergy*, constitutes, in spite of the omission of the highly mystical passages, a substantial concession.

Offering practical advice to a young Christian in a letter dated May 2, 1771, Wesley manifests respect for Law: "The four volumes of *Sermons*, the *Appeals*, the *Notes*, and the extracts from Mr. Law's words and from Dr. Young, might best suit you now."[75] Also, in a letter of November, 1774, he says, "Some of the most useful [works] to believers are Law's tracts. . . ."[76] And finally, Wesley wrote to an itinerant minister, Mr. Black, about a book by Henry Alline, July 13, 1783, "I have sent you . . . two volumes of Mr. Law's works, which contain all that Mr. Alline would teach, if he could; only it is the gold purged from the dross."[77]

These brief comments by Wesley as he neared the end of his life say something of the esteem in which he continued to hold Law in spite of their differences and in spite of the alleged error into which Law had fallen. There must have been an abiding influence and irresistible appeal in the life and works of the Non-juror to elicit such remarks.

Hobhouse contends that the pernicious influence that Wesley earlier ascribed to Law was caused by Law's association with the Moravian doctrine of "stillness." This doctrine taught that for "anyone who had attained a perfect faith and assurance of salvation, it was well to live a life of silent devotion, avoiding attendance at church and at the Lord's supper, and even the reading of the Scriptures."[78] One can understand Wesley's aversion to any such fanatical attachments in Law. However, Green's summary of the connection between the two comes much nearer to the whole truth. He says that Wesley was attracted to Law by the latter's "ethical

ideal"; that when Wesley was "converted" in 1738, he sought recourse
to the formularies and sacraments of the church and felt a mounting
aversion to the new mystical tendencies in Law. In any event, Wesley
continued to "love and reverence Law to the end, without com-
promising doctrinal differences." This balanced view circumvents
that of the extremists who insist upon driving a permanent wedge
between them. Wesley, both early and late, commended the devotional value of Law's works. And since Wesley had been aided most in
his search for spiritual fulfillment by the intense fervor and penetrating insights of the Non-juror, one is convinced that Wesley's debt to
Law was enduring.

IV *Law's Place in the Literature of Devotion*

As Willard Sperry maintains, "The Biblical quality of our religion
has been best perpetuated in its devotional literature, through which
its indubitable saints speak to us about the life of the soul."[79] This
literature bears some relationship to the times out of which it grew,
but even more it is as independent of history as books can be. It does
not usually contain much formal theology, nor does one need more
than a minimum of critical apparatus to understand it. Yet one turns
to it constantly for its self-revelation and promise of renewed life in
the soul.

Although the tradition of devotional literature in the western
world goes back to early beginnings and continues without interrup-
tion, the principal themes and worshipful manner of the contributors
do not change. The moral and spiritual dilemmas that man faces; the
crises of human spirits locked in combat with hostile forces and the
longing for deliverance; the instinct of the heart to reach out for
outside help; the desire to understand one's self and to achieve
identification with a spiritual Father—all are concerns which lend to
devotional literature in general a kind of timelessness and geographi-
cal transcendence.

Any serious review of that substantial body of religious literature
which is concerned primarily with God's intimate dealings with the
human soul must take into account the devotional writings of
William Law, for he spoke as clearly and forcefully concerning the
ways and means of spiritual worship as did St. Augustine or Lancelot
Andrewes or John Bunyan. He addressed himself as surely to the
universal needs of the soul inquiring into the ways of God as did
Donne or St. Theresa or Tauler.

When one recognizes that the devotional writers spoke out of the intuitive springs of their hearts, the homogeneous character of their writings is not hard to understand. Law, it is true, was influenced in his spiritual interpretations of Christian doctrine by the mystics and was familiar with numerous writings of the Church Fathers, but one has not really listened to this eighteenth-century Non-juror until he has heard his own refined, original counsel for spiritual improvement. Law may have been derivative in his elaborations of abstruse mystical theory, but his exhortations to worship, his counsel for personal spiritual betterment, and his pleas for the heart to cease from idolatry and to abandon itself to a beneficent Being, even though they sounded very much like many of his forerunners in Christian devotion, were distinctive.

Law's place in the established tradition of devotional writing becomes all the more noteworthy when one recognizes the intellectual and spiritual stature of those who belong to that company. Men like Thomas à Kempis, Jeremy Taylor, and St. Francis de Sales are more than religious bigots who contend for a one-sided view of life. They are, on the whole, intellectual giants who wrestle for the minds as well as the hearts of men and who seek to nourish and cultivate both spiritual and intellectual well-being.

Often the brilliant minds of the devotionalists are honed by academic training. In addition to the cumulative knowledge that they gain through formal study, they possess unusual insight into the place that man holds as a moral, sentient, responsible human being. They take into account the true nature of man without flattery or hopeless disparagement. Bold in speech, they never underestimate the evil and chicanery in man's nature and are, consequently, emphatic about the need for moral and spiritual renovation. William Law's intense piety, his daring and forthright manner, and his vitality and magnanimity of spirit reveal that he, too, perceived clearly the life-forces that strive for ascendency in the human heart.

Truth for the devotional writer was more than a set of beautiful, soft-spoken platitudes. Personal righteousness was not meant to be coetaneous with worldly success; happiness was not envisioned as mere release from earthly poverty or personal inhibitions. Truth and happiness, rather, consisted in individual belief in a way of life which proclaimed self-denial, acceptance of divine grace, and emulation of the life of Christ. Recognizing fully the adversaries in the human will, the devotionalists admitted no compromise and recognized no ranks or favors, but held before the one who persisted in righteous practice the promise of divine approval and reward.

In several ways Law grew out of the soil of the eighteenth-century thought; also, his association with the Evangelical Movement was particularly noteworthy. Nevertheless, in other ways he stands apart from the thought currents of his day. He stood in awe before the mystery of the universe against those who regarded it as a machine. He was not deluded into thinking that new solutions were always mandatory for old problems. As Non-juror and semi-recluse, he turned from active participation in world affairs; yet he was no idle dreamer. His paramount interests lay in the spiritual welfare of his contemporaries, and he wrote to correct their errors in spiritual faith and practice. He saw very little meaning in the world apart from spiritual-mindedness and perfection of life.

To him, reasonableness in religion must mean entire devotion to God. Law stood out against the anemic pronouncements of the Latitudinarians, the profligacy of the libertines, the misuse of reason by the Deists, and the denial of miracles by the Socinians. As a critic of the moral laxness of the times, he gave new hope to that remnant of the church that was dismayed to see the loosening of the church's grip upon human conduct.

Both the life and writings of Law reveal a man of pronounced religious conviction. Whenever he believed a current practice to be inconsistent with Christian precept, he denounced it boldly. He believed, moreover, that the same righteous goal toward which he strove was within reach of anyone who would travel the disciplinary path leading to it. If Law appeared dogmatic, it was because he believed so earnestly in the reality and permanence of his vision. Sometimes his dogmatism appears in his repetitious manner. Whether he discusses the composition of the world, enumerates the arguments against natural religion, or comments upon the nature of the sacraments, his exploring of the many-sided aspects of his subject often leads him to a repetitiousness that accentuates the intensity with which he expounds upon the subject.[80]

The goal that Law holds continually before the reader in both the early and late writings is perfection. That such a high standard caused many of his followers to become discouraged when they failed to measure up to it does not necessarily brand Law as an apostle of gloom; rather, it may be more a tribute to his sensitive idealism which was acutely aware of the gap between what man is and what he ought to be. Moreover, Law was supremely confident that the perfection which he enjoined is attainable when one enlists his will whole-heartedly and engages in devotional activity.

Even Law's controversial writings reveal a preoccupation with pious rules and spiritual conduct. But it is primarily in the works of pure devotion that he really excels in the art of spiritual persuasion. He writes under the impelling necessity of helping professing Christians to seek a life of communion with God. He expatiates upon the great themes of the devotional tradition. His spiritual tone is produced and maintained by adhering faithfully to the basic religious assumptions of the Christian church. He is principally traditional; that is, his correspondence to the mainstream of devotional writers is more striking than his distinguishing features. The kinship he holds with other great devotional writers is significant enough to grant him a prominent place among them.

Law may not have touched many new themes in his devotional materials, but everything that he wrote bore the unmistakable stamp of his own individuality. His treatment of prayer, for instance, was remarkably refined. Although he recognized the need for times and forms of prayer, prayer for him meant realignment with God's purposes. Prayer is far more than plying the mind of a reluctant God. When Law speaks of prayer and devotion as being a life, he means just that. The resumption of new life derived from God gives the worshiper a new orientation. Prayer becomes thinking God's thoughts, sharing God's nature, and living in accord with God's will. Persons like Caroline Spurgeon, who have been charmed by the mystical ardor and imaginative quality of *The Spirit of Prayer*, have been impressed repeatedly with the exalted conception of prayer that breathes in Law's works.

Even when Law becomes affected by the teachings of the mystics, he continues to produce works that fit into the devotional pattern. The themes and tone are not altered substantially. Admittedly, Law's emphasis upon being completely controlled by the Spirit of God is more pronounced in the later works; finding a unitive experience with God becomes more prominent, therefore, in *The Spirit of Love, The Spirit of Prayer*, and *The Way to Divine Knowledge*. But Law's shift toward an intuitive perception of God indicates his increased determination to find permanent, true reality through exploration of subjective experience. For him, the devotional activity was never complete until the seeker had been purged, illuminated by the spirit of a new life, and made one with the Eternal Spirit. By denying his own will and accepting the divine will he was controlled by a new center of being. Faith meant new life, and new life meant to participate directly in the life of God. Devotional activity began, therefore, with man's reinstatement into the pristine status which he knew before he fell from grace and it continued by constant union with the divine life, which was ever accessible to the believer.

Even when Law was censured for his mysticism or alleged universalism or for supplying an extra-biblical rationale for the Christian faith, few doubted that his devotional intensity persisted to the end. In fact, when Law's mystical flame burns most brightly, he appears most confident of his message. Few writers have sung more charmingly of the theme of divine love or of the Spirit-filled life.

The mystical features that characterize Law really exist in varying degrees among numerous writers of devotion. While his mystical language at times sounds rather unusual, Law confined himself to precepts of devotion that could be experienced by any sincere, believing, devout soul. He may not have denied the possibility of such suprasensory experiences as were professed by Jacob Boehme or Marjery Kemp, but he did not make these the norm of Christian experience. The ineffable, noetic qualities of the highest mystical state were never claimed by Law or enjoined upon his readers.

Not the least of reasons for Law's deserving a place among the distinguished writers of devotional prose literature is the impression he has made upon other influential minds. Even those who have complained of the gloom and austerity of the early works or chided him for rummaging in the strange bypaths of the Christian faith in the later writings have paid tribute to his intellectual power, his incisiveness, and his piety. The influence that he has exerted upon the Church of England and leaders of the Evangelical Movement can hardly be measured, but, conservatively, it is impressive.

Of one thing we may be sure. Anyone who will read at length in Law will be arrested by his direct, pungent language. Inasmuch as piety for him begins in the wellsprings of desire, he strikes sharply at the paralysis of will in the believer. Men do not live righteously, he contends, simply because they do not want to. He admits no carefully plotted excuses for failure in devotion. His abrupt, probing manner may invite angry retorts from those who contend that their lapses in devotion are mere inadvertencies rather than deliberate failures. Whether or not one agrees with Law's views, this shock-treatment method of penetrating the camouflaged defenses of the Christian is at least attention-getting. The characteristic method used by many of the devotionalists may have been to woo the reader, but Law belonged more to that variety of pious souls who believed that bold self-analysis provided the long first step toward spiritual recovery.

One senses in all of Law's writings a dominant desire to picture the contrast between the church and the world, or, as Leslie Stephen puts it, "between the morality taught by Jesus of Nazareth and the morality practiced by a Walpole or a Warburton."[81] Hopkinson compares *Christian Perfection* with Augustine's *Confessions* by saying that the latter was addressed to God, the former to man—that Law wrestles for the souls of men through sincere proclamation of his own convictions.[82] He possessed "the stuff of which reformers are made." Without identifying himself formally with any church group, he served well believers both within and without organized church ranks. His later treatises have not yet held the spotlight of attention as much as the earlier works, but even here Law proclaims clearly that God is love, that man is a fallen creature and ought to will a reunion with Him if he is to live happily and well.

Notes and References

Preface
1. For a significant study of early devotional prose literature see Helen C. White, *English Devotional Literature, 1600-1640* (Madison: University of Wisconsin Press, 1931); also see Helen V. McHugh, "English Devotional Prose,1200-1535," Diss. Stanford, 1948, for a similar study of early English literature.

Chapter One
1. John H. Overton, *William Law, Non-Juror and Mystic* (London: Longmans, Green, and Co., 1881), p. 5. Hereafter cited as Overton.
2. Law's appointment as Sizar meant that he was to receive from the University an allowance toward college expenses in exchange for "certain menial tasks." See Colin Wilson, "William Law" in *Religion and the Rebel* (Boston: Houghton Mifflin Co., 1957), p. 209.
3. See Stephen Hobhouse, "William Law's Sources" in *Selected Mystical Writings of William Law* (New York: Harper and Brothers, 1948), pp. 361-67. Hobhouse here presents the likely sources for Law's ideas based on the latter's own statements in his published works, parallels between his and other writings, statements of John Byrom in the *Journals,* and the more than six hundred books left in the library at King's Cliffe, which Law presumably read.
4. The Non-juror believed in the Divine Right and ordination of the monarchy and the indefeasibility of hereditary right; he also believed that God commanded passive resistance and obedience to the king. The original Non-jurors were Tories called Jacobites because they were supporters of deposed James II.
5. Christopher Walton, *Notes and Materials for an Adequate Biography of . . . William Law* (London: privately printed, 1854), p. 344. Hereafter cited as Walton.
6. There is conjecture about Law's activities after he left Cambridge. Most accounts say that he went to London and officiated as Curate at St. Mary's Church in the Strand; however, Hobhouse cites evidence that Law held the curacy at Haslingfield before he became a Non-juror. Hobhouse also holds to the 1723 date as marking the beginning of the Law-Gibbon association, although Overton and others prefer 1727.

WILLIAM LAW

7. Robert N. Flew, *The Idea of Perfection in Christian Theology* (London: Oxford University Press, 1934), p. 299. Hereafter cited as Flew.

8. Law not only gave freely of his own fortune to charity, but he also persuaded his companions at King's Cliffe to give of theirs. Mrs. Hutcheson's annual income was estimated at two to three thousand pounds, Miss Gibbon's at about one thousand. Overton tells us that of the three thousand pounds only three hundred were spent annually on the household expenses; the rest was given to the poor.

9. Walton, pp. 497 ff.

10. The rector, Mr. Piedmont, was irked at the alleged "mistaken benevolence" at King's Cliffe and preached against it openly on occasion. A letter found among Miss Gibbon's papers in Law's handwriting directed to the justices of the peace expressed regret for any offense and suggested that Law and his companions might go elsewhere if their efforts were not appreciated. Afterward, the discontent seems to have evaporated and the workers continued to help the needy.

11. Overton, p. 444.

12. Overton, p. 502.

13. John H. Overton and Frederic Relton, *A History of the English Church from the Accession of George I to the End of the Eighteenth Century, 1714–1800* (New York: The Macmillan Co., 1906), p. 1. Hereafter cited as Overton and Relton.

14. William Kemp Clarke, *Eighteenth-Century Piety* (New York: The Macmillan Co., 1944) p. 28.

15. George M. Trevelyan, *English Social History* (London: Longmans & Co., 1942), p. 353.

16. Henry O. Wakeman, *An Introduction to the History of the Church of England* (London: Rivingtons, 1949), p. 423. Francis Paget in *The Churchman's Companion in the Closet* (New York: Stanford, 1853), pp. iii-iv, lists private devotions from the works of Laud, Andrewes, Ken Hickes, Kettlewell, Spinckes, and other divines of the Church of England as among the few devotional works from the seventeenth century which continued to be in demand during the eighteenth century.

17. Norman Sykes, *The English Religious Tradition* (London: SCM Press, 1953), p. 60.

18. Ronald A. Knox, *Enthusiasm* (New York: Oxford University Press, 1950), p. 244.

19. Wakeman, p. 419.

20. John M. Creed, *Religious Thought in the Eighteenth Century* (Cambridge: The University Press, 1934), p. xviii.

21. Berkeley implied a belief in God and spiritual interpretation of all reality. Butler argued for theism and the moral purpose of the world through a survey of experience. Hume, by pursuing the principles of Locke and Berkeley to their logical conclusions, showed the need for a deeper basis for religious faith than the arguments being used.

22. Creed, p. xxii.

23. Mark Pattison, "Tendencies of Religious Thought in England, 1688–1750," in *Essays and Reviews* (London: Longman, Green, 1860), p. 290.

24. Overton and Relton, p. 4.

25. William Law, *The Works of the Reverend William Law* (London: J. Richardson, 1762, rpt. London: G. Moreton, 1892–93), I, II, 1–54. Hereafter cited as *Works*.

Chapter Two

1. "A Bibliography of Some Devotional Books Printed by the Earliest Printers," *Trans. of the Bibl. Soc.*, VII (1904), 164.

2. "A Subject Analysis of Early Imprints for Every Tenth Year from 1480–1640," *Huntington Library Quarterly (HLQ)*, I (1937–38), 417–19.

3. Helen C. White, *English Devotional Literature, 1600–1640*, (Madison: University of Wisconsin Press, 1931). Hereafter cited as White.

4. The *Cambridge Bibliography of English Literature*, II, 845–60, lists more than seventy authors and their works under the caption, "Religious Prose: Devotional and Controversial, 1660–1800." Included are religious writings of almost every kind. Also, F. A. Gasquet in his bibliography of devotional books printed in the first few decades after the introduction of printing does not hold to a consistent and strict classification.

5. White, p. 163.

6. Helen McHugh, "English Devotional Prose, 1200–1535," Diss. Stanford, 1948, p. 10. Hereafter cited as McHugh.

7. See Erwin P. Rudolph, "A Study of the Religious Thought of William Law (1686–1761)," Diss. Illinois, 1962, pp. 7–37.

8. Overton, pp. 48–49. This is a quotation from Bishop Wilson's letter to Elizabeth Hastings, dated Warrington, September 13, 1729.

9. *Works*, III, [iii]-iv.

10. Overton, pp. 111, 119.

11. Walton, pp. 345, 346, leaves blank the space for "coffeehouses." Hobhouse declares, after his analysis of the original autograph of the eighteen rules in the Walton collection in Dr. William's Library, that the words "public houses" (i.e., coffeehouses) belong in the blank. See Hobhouse, p. 384.

12. Edward Pusey, trans., *The Confessions of St. Augustine* (London: T. Nelson and Sons, 1937), pp. 104–214. The *Short-Title Catalogue of English Books, 1475–1640*, pp. 22–23, lists forty-eight English translations of St. Augustine's works.

13. The *Short-Title Catalogue* lists forty-six English translations of Thomas à Kempis.

14. François Fenelon, *Christian Perfection*, trans. Mildred Stillman (New York: Harper and Brothers 1947). Law seldom refers to Fenelon (1651–1715), but his library at King's Cliffe contained a well-worn copy of the works by that French writer.

15. Allan Ross, *Saint Francis de Sales and the Introduction to the Devout Life* (London: Burns, Oates & Washbourne, 1925), pp. 5-6.

16. *Works*, III, 7.

17. R. N. Flew, pp. 293, 301.

18. *Works*, III, 13.

19. John Donne, *Devotions Upon Emergent Occasions*, ed. John Sparrow (Cambridge: University Press, 1923), pp. vii, 5.

20. *Works*, III, 25.

21. Ibid., 27.

22. Ibid., 215-16.

23. McHugh, p. 122.

24. James Morton, trans., *The Nun's Rule* (London: Alexander Moring, 1905).

25. John H. Newman, trans., *The Private Devotions of Lancelot Andrewes* (New York: G. H. Richmond & Co., 1897), pp. 137-38.

26. François Fenelon, *Christian Perfection*, trans. Mildred Stillman (New York: Harper and Brothers, 1947), p. 4.

27. Aurelius Augustine, *The City of God*, trans., John Healy (London: J. M. Dent & Sons, 1942), Part III, p. 31.

28. Susanna Winkworth, trans., *Theologia Germanica* (London: Victor Gollancz, 1951), p. 146.

29. *Works*, IV, 53.

30. Ibid., 58-59.

31. Ibid., 63-65.

32. Ibid., 77.

33. Ibid., 188, 107.

34. *Works*, III, 59.

35. Ibid., 68.

36. Ibid., 250.

37. Julia Wedgwood, "William Law, the English Mystic of the Eighteenth Century," *Contemporary Review* (1877), p. 92.

38. *Works*, III, 170-71. "The Absolute Unlawfulness . . ." was originally prepared as a separate pamphlet and subsequently included as a part of *Christian Perfection*. Collier's work was entitled *A Short View of the Immorality and Profaneness of the English Stage* (1698). See Allardyce Nicoll, *A History of the English Drama* (Cambridge: University Press, 1952), II, 14. Here it is pointed out that Colley Cibber's *The Non-Jurors*, first presented in 1717, and quite popular in the 1720s, may have helped to prompt Law's comments on the stage.

39. *Works*, II, 144.

40. John Dennis, *The Stage Defended from Scripture, Reason, Experience, and the Common Sense of Mankind, for Two-Thousand Years, Occasion'd by Mr. Law's Late Pamphlet Against Stage Entertainment* (London: N. Blandford, 1726).

41. *Works*, III, 179. There is no evidence that Law ever saw the inside of a

playhouse, but he had plenty of opportunity when he lived in the Gibbon household.

42. *Works*, III, 180.
43. *The Vision of God* (London: Longmans & Co., 1931), p. ix. This series of lectures traces the concept of the vision of God from its antecedents in Jewish and pagan thought to New Testament writers who insist on primacy in worship through a succession of those who emphasized the importance of contemplative prayer.
44. *Holy Living and Holy Dying* (London: William Pickering, 1864), pp. 128–51.
45. *The Plain Man's Pathway to Heaven* (London: Robert Dexter, 1601), pp. 191–92.
46. *Works*, III, 33.
47. Helen White, *Tudor Books of Private Devotion* (Madison: University of Wisconsin Press, 1951), p. 5.
48. *Middle Class Culture in Elizabethan England* (Chapel Hill: University of N. Carolina Press, 1935), pp. 38–39.
49. A. C. Southern, *Elizabethan Recusant Prose, 1559–1582* (London: Sands, 1950), pp. 38–39.
50. Thomas Becon, *Prayers and Other Pieces*, ed. for The Parker Society by John Ayre (Cambridge: University Press, 1844), pp. 2–70.
51. Ibid., 74.
52. Richard Baxter, *The Saints' Everlasting Rest*, ed. by Benjamin Fawcett (New York: American Tract Society, 1758), pp. 428 ff.
53. *Works*, III, 196.
54. *Works*, IV, 135.
55. Ibid., 189.
56. Ibid., 131–32.
57. Ibid., 136.
58. Ibid., 137.
59. Ibid., 146–47.
60. Ibid., 258–59.
61. S. H. Gem, "The Mysticism of William Law: a Study," *Spectator*, CXLII (July 25, 1914), p. 138.
62. *Works*, III, 17. Also, see *Works*, IV, 269.
63. Edward Pusey, trans., *The Confessions of St. Augustine* (London: T. Nelson and Sons, 1937), pp. 176–77.
64. Thomas à Kempis, *The Imitation of Christ* (London: Medici Society, 1930), p. 163.
65. Nicholas Malebranche, *Dialogues on Metaphysics and on Religion* (New York: Macmillan Co., 1923), p. 43. Malebranche attempted to effect a synthesis between the Augustinian, or Neo-Platonic doctrine of ideas, and the teaching of Descartes.
66. *The Plain Man's Pathway to Heaven* (London: Robert Dexter, 1601), pp. 191–92.

67. *History of English Thought in the Eighteenth Century* (New York: G. P. Putnam's Sons, 1876), I, 163. Hereafter cited as *History of English Thought.*

68. *Works*, IV, 19-20.

69. Louis L. Martz, *The Poetry of Meditation* (New Haven: Yale University Press, 1954), p. 21.

70. *Works*, IV, 271.

71. Ibid., 271-72.

72. "William Law and His Influence on His Age," *Contemporary Review*, VI, 133, 136.

73. Edward Gibbon, *The Autobiography of Edward Gibbon*, ed. Oliphant Smeaton (London: Dent, n.d.), p. 18.

74. *Works*, III, 133.

75. McHugh, p. 185.

Chapter Three

1. The Anglican Church had been charged with unlawful appointment of bishops in replacement of Non-jurors. Hoadley denied the rights of the Church to legislate or interpret spiritual matters. He contended that the Church was only a witness in matters of faith, not a judge. Although Hoadley was a bishop of the Church of England, he was disavowing the views he was supposed to hold in his episcopal capacity. His position was similar to that of Thomas Lieber, or Erastus (1524-83), who popularized the notion that the Christian Church had no rights of jurisdiction or authority to excommunicate. Hoadley's view was occasionally termed "Erastian." See A. S. Turberville, *English Men and Manners in the Eighteenth Century* (Oxford: The Clarendon Press, 1926), p. 303.

2. *History of English Thought*, I, 156.

3. *Works*, I, 22.

4. Ibid., 78.

5. Matthew 18: 15-18; I Corinthians 5; I Timothy 1:19.

6. *Works*, V, 13.

7. Overton, p. 121.

8. Alexander Whyte, *Characters and Characteristics of William Law* (London: Hodder and Stoughton, 1893), p. xxi.

9. Bernard Mandeville, *The Fable of the Bees*, ed. F. B. Kaye (Oxford: The Clarendon Press, 1924), p. xlviii.

10. A. Owen Aldridge, "Polygamy and Deism," *Journal of English and Germanic Philology (JEGP)*, XLVIII, pp. 343-60.

11. *Works*, III, 98-105.

12. Ralph Inge, *Studies in English Mystics* (London: J. Murray, 1906), pp. 169-70.

13. Stephen Hobhouse, *Selected Mystical Writings of William Law* (New York: Harper and Brothers, 1948), p. 366. Hereafter cited as Hobhouse.

14. Samuel G. Hefelbower, "Deism Historically Defined," *American Journal of Theology*, XXIV (1920), 220.

15. Mark Pattison, "Tendencies of Religious Thought in England, 1688–1750," in *Essays and Reviews* (London: Longman, 1860), p. 290.

16. *Works*, II, iv. John Sterling in the prefatory advertisement.

17. *History of English Thought*, II, 42.

18. *Works*, II, 138.

19. Wakeman, p. 419.

20. *History of English Thought*, II, 396.

21. *History of English Thought*, I, 163 and Hopkinson's *About William Law: a Running Commentary on His Work* (London: Society for Publication of Christian Knowledge, 1948), p. 13, hereafter cited as Hopkinson.

22. In the same year, after Trapp wrote a reply, Law countered with *Some Animadversions upon Dr. Trapp's Late Reply*. He reiterated his earlier arguments and refuted Trapp's charge that Law was connected with the Quakers, even though at times he equated religious enthusiasm with true religious feeling. Law here is more unqualified in his praise of enthusiasm than in *Christian Regeneration* (1739), where he warns against enthusiasm which seems to be indecorous or violent.

23. *Works*, VI, 47.

24. *Works*, VIII, 139.

25. II Timothy 1:9–10.

26. *Works*, V, 137.

27. Hans L. Martenson, *Jacob Boehme*, trans. T. Rhys Evans (London: Hodder and Stoughton, 1885), pp. 52–76; also see G. W. Allen, "Boehme," *Encyclopedia of Religion and Ethics*, II, 778–84.

28. *Works*, VIII, 250.

29. W. H. Lewis, ed., *The Letters of C. S. Lewis* (London: Geoffrey Bless Ltd., 1966), p. 143.

30. *Selected Mystical Writings of William Law*, p. 249.

31. Hopkinson, p. 99.

32. *Works*, VII, 83.

33. *Works*, VI, 99.

34. Walton, 601–602.

35. Boehme is not the only precedent for such teaching. Susanna Winkworth, trans., *The Theologia Germanica* (London: Victor Gollancz, 1951), pp. 190–92, speaks of the "seed of God" which brings forth fruit in the soul (new birth). Also, Tauler writes of the birth of God in man as similar to that which took place in Mary.

36. Hobhouse, p. 299, points out that Law's view was similar to that of the early Greek Fathers, and of Irenaeus (ca. 150 A.D.) in particular. He cites the four volumes of Irenaeus in the King's Cliffe Library as evidence of Law's familiarity with that writer. Irenaeus taught that it was through Christ's obedience and perfect resistance to temptation more than by his death that man's union with God was made possible.

37. *Works*, VIII, 45.
38. Walton, p. 363.
39. Rufus M. Jones, *The Luminous Trail* (New York: Macmillan Co., 1947), p. 130.
40. Walton, p. 358.
41. *Works*, IX, 225. The Non-jurors of the seventeenth century had been concerned with reunion with the Catholic Church. There was also interest in the possibility of reuniting with the Eastern Orthodox Church, especially when negotiations for reunion with Rome failed. See Walter Adeney, *The Greek and Eastern Churches* (New York: Charles Scribner's Sons, 1908), p. 324.
42. *Works*, IX, 97.
43. Ibid., [5].
44. Ibid., 179. Letter XI is captioned, "To a Person Burdened with Inward and Outward Troubles." The entire collection of Law's letters appears in the *Works*, IX, 177–214.

Chapter Four

1. *Mysticism in English Literature* (Cambridge: University Press, 1913), p. 6.
2. William K. Fleming, *Mysticism in Christianity* (London: R. Scott, 1913), p. 1.
3. Rufus Jones, *Spiritual Reformers in the Sixteenth and Seventeenth Centuries* (London: Macmillan and Co., Ltd., 1914), p. xxviii.
4. *Christian Mysticism* (New York: Charles Scribner's Sons, 1915), p. 3 hereafter cited as Inge.
5. Evelyn Underhill, *Practical Mysticism* (New York: E. P. Dutton and Co., 1915), p. 3.
6. Henri Bremond, *A Literary History of Religious Thought in France from the Wars of Religion Down to Our Own Time.* (London: Society for Publication of Christian Knowledge, 1928–1936), II, 431–32.
7. Gerald W. Bullett, *The English Mystics* (London: Michael Joseph, 1950), pp. 13–14.
8. Caroline Spurgeon, *Mysticism in English Literature*, p. 3.
9. Ibid., 6.
10. W. K. Fleming, *Mysticism in Christianity*, p. 17.
11. Ibid., 18–19. Evelyn Underhill in *Mysticism* (London: Methuen & Co. Ltd., 1911), pp. 213–452, gives a more elaborate system of steps as follows: (1) awakening of self, or awakening of transcendental consciousness; (2) purification of self; (3) illumination; (4) voices and visions; (5) introversion (recollection, quiet contemplation); (6) ecstasy (alleged attainment of the Absolute). The last three are reached only by great mystics; the first three are normal to the spiritual life.
12. Inge, p. 11.
13. Ibid.

14. Fleming, *Mysticism in Christianity*, pp. 8–25.
15. Inge, p. 14.
16. *The Varieties of Religious Experience* (London: Longmans, Green, & Co., 1903), pp. 380–81.
17. Inge, p. 16.
18. J. B. Green, *John Wesley and William Law* (London: Epworth Press, 1945), p. 178.
19. Hobhouse, 361–67. Law mentions most of these writers in his second reply to Dr. Trapp as constituting much of his reading. See *Works*, VI, 203–204. The last two named, Origen and Irenaeus, are not considered mystics.
20. Francis Okeley, *Memoirs of Behmen* (1780), p. xiii.
21. *Works*, VI, 203–204.
22. *Works*, VII, 195. Born of humble parents near Gorlitz, Germany, in 1775, Jacob Boehme gave little indication of the genius that was to unfold later on. He tended cattle at an early age, gained some elementary schooling at the nearby town of Seidenberg, and at thirteen became a shoemaker's apprentice.
23. Walton, p. 26. According to Stephen Hobhouse in "Fides et Ratio," *Journal of Theological Studies*, XXXVIII, pp. 350–68, Dr. George Cheyne brought "Fides et Ratio" and Law together.
24. These writings were deemed revolutionary and heretical by the powerful Pastor Gregorious Richter and led for a time to open censure and temporary banishment from the community. Boehme was later exonerated and returned to his home.
25. See Jacob Boehme, *The Works of Jacob Behmen, the Teutonic Theosopher . . . with Figures Illustrating His Principles, Left by the Rev. William Law* (London: Richardson, 1764–81), 4 Vol. 1 contains the "Aurora" and "The Three Principles"; Vol. II: *The High and Deep Searching of the Threefold Life of Man*; Vol III: *The Mysterium Magnum*, or an explanation of the first book of Moses; Vol. IV discusses such subjects as "The Signature of All Things," "Of the Election of Grace," "The Way to Christ," "Of the Four Complexions," and "The Supper."
26. Jacob Boehme, *The Way to Christ*, trans. John Stoudt (New York: Harper & Brothers, 1947), p. xxxvi.
27. J. B. Green, *John Wesley and William Law* (London: Epworth Press, 1945), p. 98. Hereafter cited as Green.
28. Hopkinson, p. 84.
29. Ibid., 73.
30. Alexander Whyte, *Characters and Characteristics of William Law*, p. xlii.
31. *Works*, VII, 24.
32. *Works*, VIII, 43–44.
33. Ibid., 54.
34. *Works*, VII, 226–227.

35. Ibid., 98.
36. *Works*, VIII, 45.
37. *Works*, VII, 190.
38. Jan Van Ruysbroeck, *The Adornment of the Spiritual Marriage*, trans. C. A. Wynschenk Dom (London: J. M. Dent & Sons, 1916), p. 62. The idea of God's birth in the depths of man's soul is the aim of all mystical practice.
39. *Works*, VIII, 97.
40. Law makes it plain that he believes Boehme has merely uncovered some of the latent truths of the Scriptures. Law also had a striking precedent in Dionysius the Areopagite who expounded upon the implications of certain biblical passages. The latter believed revealed religion had the insuperable job of making known incomprehensible mysteries.
41. *Works*, VII, 160.
42. *Works*, VIII, 64.
43. Ibid., 124.
44. *Theologia Germanica* (London: Victor Gollancz, 1951), p. 315.
45. François Fenelon, *Christian Perfection*, trans. Mildred Stillman (New York: Harper and Brothers, 1947), pp. 192-93.
46. Jan Van Ruysbroeck, p. 27.
47. *Works*, VII, 35-36.
48. Ibid., 45.
49. Ibid., 151-52.
50. Ibid., 60.
51. Ibid., 95.
52. Ibid., 97.
53. Ibid., 190.
54. Ibid., 126.
55. Ibid., 120.
56. Ibid., 128.
57. It is interesting to note, however, that the Evangelical preacher George Whitefield read *The Spirit of Prayer* and refused to condemn its teachings. He commented, "Though Law wrote many chimerical things, he says many things truly noble. The sun has its spots, and so do the best of men." See Stephen Hobhouse, *William Law and Eighteenth-Century Quakerism*, p. 322.
58. Hopkinson, p. 54.
59. *Works*, VII, 8.
60. *Works*, VIII, 57-60.
61. *Religion and the Rebel* (Boston: Houghton Mifflin Co., 1957), p. 217.
62. *Works*, VII, 47.
63. Ibid., 48.
64. *Works*, VIII, 125, 127.
65. *Works*, VII, 100.
66. Ibid., 209.

67. Ibid., 180–81.
68. *Works*, VIII, [3].

Chapter Five

1. George P. Krapp, *The Rise of English Literary Prose* (New York: Oxford University Press, 1915), p. 3.
2. McHugh, p. 300.
3. White, pp. 236 ff.
4. *The Cambridge History of English Literature*, IX, 323.
5. "William Law," *Studies of English Mystics*, pp. 124–25.
6. Edward Gibbon, *The Autobiography of Edward Gibbon* (London: Macmillan & Co., 1930), pp. 17–18.
7. *Religion and the Rebel*, p. 212.
8. Henri Talon, *William Law: A Study in Literary Craftsmanship* (London: Rockliff, 1948), p. 32. Hereafter cited as Talon.
9. *The Cambridge History of English Literature*, IX, 359.
10. *Works*, IV, 96.
11. *Works*, VIII, 46. Law had the habit of capitalizing nouns and other key words and italicizing for emphasis. He also placed commas copiously throughout the text wherever the sentence contained a logical pause. These peculiarities, not unfamiliar to the eighteenth-century public, may be somewhat distracting to the modern reader who is more used to open punctuation. They are, however, reproduced throughout the quotations in this study as a part of the uniqueness of Law's style.
12. See *Works*, IV, 101–102, for an illustration of this technique.
13. *Works*, III, 235.
14. Ibid., 245.
15. See *Works*, VIII, 129–30, for illustrations of this type of sentence.
16. See *Works*, VII, 122–23, for illustrations.
17. See *Works*, VII, 46, 47, for illustrations.
18. *Works*, IV, 152.
19. *Works*, VII, 127.
20. *Works*, IV, 100.
21. *Works*, VIII, 51.
22. *Works*, VI, 5.
23. *Works*, IV, 15.
24. See Benjamin Boyce, *The Theophrastus Character in England to 1642* (Cambridge: Harvard University Press, 1947). Although the English debt to Theophrastus is obvious, several influences contributed to the ready acceptance of this literary type: the popular verse satire and epigrams of the late sixteenth century; the medieval allegorical tradition, the historically familiar *descriptio personae* device, and the "literature of estates" as found in Brandt's *Ship of Fools*. After enjoying a comparatively brief popularity, the character was absorbed in the eighteenth-century essay and novel.
25. *Works*, III, 139.

26. Ibid. Some other characters included in *Christian Perfection* are Philo, the virtuoso; Eusebius, a grammarian and parish minister; Julia, a novel-reading widow, and Credula, a busybody. Other characters include Penitens, a noble tradesman; Serena, a lady of leisure; Cognatus, a man in holy orders; and Mundanus, a man of parts. A few of these may have had living counterparts. For example, Miranda, the ideal woman, allegedly referred to Miss Hester Gibbon. Identification of the originals is speculation, although most of the characters probably represented *types* of people more than specific individuals.

27. *History of English Thought*, II, 401.

28. Hopkinson, p. 55.

29. *Works*, VII, 53. *The Way to Divine Knowledge* continues the dialogue between these same personages. *The Spirit of Love* is in two parts: (1) In a Letter to a Friend, and (2) Three Dialogues between Theogenes, Eusebius, and Theophilus.

30. *Works*, VII, 115–16.

31. Talon, p. 92.

32. Mary C. Robb, "Light Against Light," Diss. Pittsburgh, 1958, pp. 254–55. The author lists nineteen known editions of *A Serious Call* before 1850.

33. J. H. Millar, *The Mid-Eighteenth Century* (New York: Charles Scribner's Sons, 1902), p. 118.

34. *Church Quarterly Review*, XLVII (January, 1899), 456, quoting from the *Apologia*, ed. of 1867, p. 6.

35. *Church Quarterly Review*, XLVII, 457.

36. William K. Clarke, *Eighteenth Century Piety* (New York: Macmillan Co., 1944), p. 23.

37. As quoted in Whyte, p. xxviii.

38. *The Descent of the Dove* (New York: Meridian Books, 1956), p. 196.

39. Rufus Jones, *The Luminous Trail* (New York: Macmillan Co., 1947), pp. 124–25.

40. William James, *The Varieties of Religious Experience* (London: Longmans, Green, and Co., 1903), p. 125.

41. Walton, p. 360.

42. Ibid., 608.

43. *Books of Faith and Power* (New York: Harper and Brothers, 1947), pp. vii, and 129.

44. *Great Christian Books* (London: SCM Press, 1945), pp. 14, 56.

45. *Religion and the Rebel*, pp. 212–13.

46. C. S. Lewis, *Letters to an American Lady*, ed. Clyde S. Kilby (Grand Rapids: W. B. Eerdmans Pub. Co., 1967), p. 43.

47. William Law, *A Serious Call to a Devout and Holy Life*, ed. John W. Meister (Philadelphia: The Westminster Press, 1955), pp. 13, 15.

48. "William Law and His Influence," *Contemporary Review*, VI, (September, 1867), 137.

49. John Byrom, *The Journal and Literary Remains.* Printed for the Chetham Society. 4 Vol., 1854–67. Byrom's diary, kept for his wife in shorthand, has been deciphered by Dr. Parkinson for the Chetham Society.

50. *Church Quarterly Review*, XXXVII (October, 1883), 204.

51. "Dr. Johnson and the Religious Problem," *English Studies*, XX, 2–6.

52. *Samuel Johnson* (New York: Harcourt Brace, 1977), p. 102.

53. *The Achievement of Samuel Johnson* (New York: Oxford University Press, 1955), p. 134.

54. "Doctor Johnson and William Law," *Publications Modern Language Association*, LXXV, 389.

55. James Boswell, *The Life of Samuel Johnson.* Intro. by Herbert Askwith. (New York: Random House, n.d.), p. 33.

56. J. L. Clifford, *Young Sam Johnson* (New York: McGraw Hill, 1955), pp. 127 ff.

57. "Dr. Johnson and William Law," *Publications Modern Language Association (PMLA)*, LXXV, 389.

58. J. B. Green, *John Wesley and William Law* (London: Epworth Press, 1945) and Eric Baker, *A Herald of the Evangelical Revival* (London: Epworth Press, 1948).

59. J. B. Green, p. 215.

60. Eric Baker, p. 187.

61. John Telford, ed., *The Letters of the Rev. John Wesley, A.M.* (London: Epworth Press, 1931), I, 161.

62. Ibid., 161–63.

63. Nehemiah Curnock, ed., *The Journal of John Wesley, A.M.* (London: Epworth Press, 1938), I, 122, 123.

64. Ibid., 467.

65. Ibid., 15.

66. Telford, I, 239.

67. Ibid., 240.

68. The Aldersgate experience refers to Wesley's spiritual awakening. Previously his life was characterized by lack of faith and defeat, but during a service at a Moravian church on Aldersgate Street he received a spiritual impetus that transformed his life and ministry. Very likely, Law's devotional directives helped to precipitate the crisis in Wesley's experience.

69. Curnock, II, 297.

70. Telford, III, 352.

71. Ibid., 332.

72. Ibid., 370.

73. *Works*, IX, 168–169.

74. Telford, IV, 105.

75. Telford, V, 241.

76. Telford, VI, 125.

77. Telford, VII, 182.

78. Stephen Hobhouse, *William Law and Eighteenth-Century Quakerism* (London: George Allen and Unwin, Ltd., 1927), p. 316.

79. *Strangers and Pilgrims: Studies in Classics of Christian Devotion* (Boston: Little, Brown and Co., 1939), pp. xi-xii.

80. An illustration of Law's repetitiousness may be illustrated by his exposition of Jacob Boehme's definition of magic. He devotes seven pages to show that magic as used by Boehme is synonymous with the will. See *Works*, VII, 212–19.

81. *History of English Thought*, II, 395.

82. Hopkinson, p. 58.

Selected Bibliography

PRIMARY SOURCES

LAW, WILLIAM. *The Works of the Reverend William Law*, M.A. London: J. Richardson, 1762; privately reprinted for G. Moreton, 1892–93. 9 vols. References throughout are to this edition.

LAW, WILLIAM. *A Serious Call to a Devout and Holy Life.* Intro. by J. V. Moldenhawer. Philadelphia: The Westminster Press, 1948.

SECONDARY SOURCES

BAKER, ERIC W. *A Herald of the Evangelical Revival.* London: The Epworth Press, 1948. Examines the basic views of Law and Boehme and how Law kindled in Wesley a passion for "an ethical ideal" that remained unimpaired.

BALDERSTON, KATHERINE C. "Doctor Johnson and William Law." *Publication Modern Language Association* (LXXXV), 382–94. Synthesizes and appraises perceptively previously expressed views of Law's influence on a leading eighteenth-century mind. Shows that Johnson and Law had broad areas of agreement and yet were opposite in temper, range of interest, and natural endowment.

BYROM, JOHN. *The Private Journal and Literary Remains of John Byrom.* Ed. Richard Parkinson. Manchester: Printed for the Chetham Society, 1854–57. 2 vols. Firsthand account of how Law appeared to some of his contemporaries.

FLEW, R. N. *The Idea of Perfection in Christian Theology.* London: Oxford University Press, 1934. Helps to place Law's idea of perfection in historical perspective by comparing it with what others have written on the subject.

GREEN, J. B. *John Wesley and William Law.* London: Epworth Press, 1945. Talks a great deal about the theological differences of Law and Wesley. Green's careful analysis of the two's association underscores how Wesley loved and reverenced Law to the end.

HOBHOUSE, STEPHEN, Ed. *Selected Mystical Writings of William Law.* New York: Harper and Brothers, 1948. Presents brief, but illuminating studies in various aspects of Law's thought. Aids an intelligent reading of the later works.

———. "Fides et Ratio, the Book Which Introduced Jacob Boehme to William Law." *Journal of Theological Studies* XXXVII (1936), 350–

68. Recounts Law's alleged initial encounter with Boehme's thought and the nature of the work that affected the former so vividly.

    William Law and Eighteenth-Century Quakerism. London: George Allen and Unwin, Ltd., 1927. Points out Law's kinship with the "inner light" movement through his emphasis on inspiration of the Spirit rather than on Scripture or the ordinances of the church. Tends to underemphasize the traditionalism in Law.

HOPKINSON, ARTHUR. *About William Law: A Running Commentary on His Work.* London: Society for Publication of Christian Knowledge, 1948. Recognizes different aspects of Law's thought: controversial, moral, mystical, theological. Sketchy, but informative.

INGE, W. R. *Christian Mysticism.* London: Methuen and Co., 1899. One of the standard sources on Christian mysticism.

McHUGH, HELEN V. "English Devotional Prose, 1200–1535." Unpublished dissertation (Stanford, 1948). A valuable supplement to Helen White's comparable study of seventeenth-century devotional prose.

MARTENSEN, HANS. *Jacob Boehme: His Life and Teaching.* Trans. T. Rhys Evans. London: Hodder and Stoughton, 1885. Provides a welcome analysis of and commentary on Jacob Boehme's numerous mystical works.

OVERTON, JOHN H. *William Law, Nonjuror and Mystic.* London: Longmans, Green, and Co., 1881. Still the best single source for Law's life and thought.

ROBB, MARY COOPER. "Light Against Light: the Literary Biography of William Law." Unpublished dissertation (Pittsburgh, 1957–58). Recognizes the essential unity of righteousness which prevails throughout Law's writings.

RUDOLPH, ERWIN P. "A Study of the Religious Thought of William Law (1686–1761)." Unpublished dissertation (Illinois, 1962). Emphasizes Law's kinship with other writers in the devotional tradition.

SPURGEON, CAROLINE. "William Law and the Mystics" in the *Cambridge History of English Literature.* Ed. A. W. Ward and A. R. Waller. New York: Putnam and Sons, 1907. IX, 350–55. A very brief, but perceptive treatment of Law's place among other outstanding mystics.

STEPHEN, LESLIE. *History of English Thought in the Eighteenth Century.* 2 vols. New York: G. P. Putnam's Sons, 1876. Helps to enlarge Law's stature by recognizing his contribution to eighteenth-century thought.

TALON, HENRI. *William Law: A Study in Literary Craftsmanship.* London: Rockliff, 1948. Attempts to establish Law's literary stature through analysis of salient features of his prose.

TIGHE, RICHARD. *A Short Account of the Life and Writings of the Late William Law.* London: The Author, 1813. Treats succinctly highlights of Law's biography. Helpful, but does not rank with Overton's biography.

UNDERHILL, EVELYN. *Mysticism.* Reprint by arrangement with E. P. Dutton and Co., Inc. Cleveland: The World Publishing Company, 1970. One of the best sourcebooks for general mystical studies.

WALKER, ARTHUR K. *William Law: His Life and Thought.* London: Society for the Publication of Christian Knowledge, 1973. Examines Law's intellectual biography, focusing upon the people whom Law knew and the writings with which he was familiar. Somewhat digressive and biased on occasion, but generally useful.

WALTON, CHRISTOPHER. *Notes and Materials for an Adequate Biography of William Law.* Privately printed. London, 1854. Although poorly organized, this contains a mass of information about Law and his mystical model, Jacob Boehme. Much biographical material is submerged in an extended footnote.

WESLEY, JOHN. *Journals of John Wesley.* Ed. Nehemiah Curnock. Standard edition. Vols. 1–2. London: The Epworth Press, 1938. Valuable in reconstructing the association of Law and Wesley and the circumstances which led to their temporary estrangement.

——. *The Letters of the Reverend John Wesley, A.M.* Ed. John Telford. Vols. 1–7. London: Epworth Press, 1931. This standard edition of Wesley's letters gives a full account of the correspondence between Law and Wesley.

WHITE, HELEN C. *English Devotional Literature, 1600–1640.* Madison: University of Wisconsin Press, 1931. An excellent survey and description of early English devotional prose. Calls attention to the different types, methods, controlling ideas, and styles.

WILSON, COLIN. "William Law" in *Religion and the Rebel.* Boston: Houghton Mifflin Co., 1957. Believes Law expressed clearly a message urgently needed in a declining civilization. Speaks appreciatively of both early and late works.

Index

Addison, Joseph, 19, 114, 116
Aldridge, A. Owen, 61
Alleged heterodoxy, 73
Ambrose, 34
Analogy of Religion (Butler), 22, 64
Anatomy of Melancholy (Burton), 117
Andrewes, Lancelot, 43, 46, 62, 109, 128
Anglican Church, 22, 52
Anne of Cleves, 43
Anselm of Canterbury, 34
Aquinas, Thomas, 34, 63
Augustine, Saint, (of Hippo), 13, 26, 30, 31, 34, 43, 52, 74, 77, 78, 86, 104, 128

Baker, Eric, 122
Balderston, Katherine, 121, 122
Bangorian Controversy, 18, 55–60
Bate, Walter Jackson, 121
Baxter, Richard, 20, 26, 43, 102
Becon, Thomas, 26, 46, 52
Berkeley, George, 21, 63, 136n21
Bernard of Clairvaux, 34, 43, 94
Birrell, Augustine, 118
Blake, William, 71, 83
Boehme, Jacob, 49, 69, 87, 88, 143n25, 95, 101, 103, 132
Bonaventura, 34, 51, 74
Book of Common Prayer, 18, 45, 56, 58
Book of Prayer and Meditation (Granada), 42
Bremond, Henri, 83
Brown, Stuart, 121
Bullett, Gerald, 83
Bunyan, John, 20, 128
Burnet, Gilbert, 21
Butler, Joseph, 18, 21, 22, 63, 65
Byrom, John, 13, 14, 120

Cambridge Platonists, 62, 85, 102
Characters of Vertues and Vices (Hall), 114
Christianity As Old As Creation (Tindal), 64
City of God (Saint Augustine), 35
Clarke, Samuel, 18, 21, 22, 55, 63
Clarke, William K., 19
Classification of early seventeenth-century devotional writing, 24
Clifford, James, 122
Collier, Jeremy, 34–35, 55
Confessions, The (Saint Augustine), 48, 133
Cousin, Victor, 83
Curnock, Nehemiah, 124, 126

Dante, 104, 105
Defoe, Daniel, 22
Deism, 63, 69; *see also* "deists"
Deistic controversy, 18, 60–66
Deists, 21, 61, 130; *see also* "deism"
Dennis, John, 39
Dent, Arthur, 41, 50
Descartes (Rene), 13, 48
Devotional influence on Samuel Johnson and John Wesley, 121–28
Devotional literature: a definition, 24–27
Devotional prose (distinguishing features), 27
Devotional prose style, 109–17
Devotional tone, 104–108
Devotions upon Emergent Occasions (Donne), 31–32, 47
Dionysius the Areopagite, 49, 69, 86, 87, 94
Directives for prayer, 45

Divine Right, 55
Donne, John, 31, 62, 128

Earl of Shaftesbury, 18
Earle, John, 114
Early works of devotion, 24–54
Eckhart, Meister, 49, 53, 69, 85, 86, 87, 101
Elaborations upon cosmology and axiology, 101–104
Emmanuel College, Cambridge, 13
Essay of Dramatic Poesy (Dryden), 116
Evangelical Movement, 130, 132

Fable of the Bees, The (Mandeville), 60–61
Fenelon, François, 13, 30, 31, 35, 49, 96, 104
Flavia, 36
Fleming, William, 84
Flew, Robert, 15, 31
Flower of Godly Prayer (Becon), 42
Four descriptive qualities of the mystical state, 85
Francis de Sales, 13, 30, 49, 53, 129
Froude, James A., 118

Gasquet, F. A., 24
Gibbon, Edward (father of the historian), 14
Gibbon, Edward (historian), 28, 53, 110, 119
Gibbon, Hester, 15, 16
Godly Meditation, A (More), 51
Grace Abounding (Bunyan), 20
Green, J. B., 89, 122, 123, 127
Guyon, Madame, 78

Hanoverians, 17
Hefelbower, Samuel, 63
Herbert of Cherbury, 63
Hilton, Walter, 36
Historical doctrines of the atonement, 76
Hoadley, Benjamin, 16, 18, 55, 57, 58, 140n1
Hobbes, Thomas, 18
Hobhouse, Stephen, 62, 72, 77, 86, 87, 121
Holy Living and *Holy Dying* (Taylor), 19, 20, 32, 124
Hopkinson, Arthur, 73, 89, 90, 102, 110, 115, 133
Hume, David, 21, 63
Hutcheson, Sarah, 15, 16
Huxley, Aldous, 90

Imitations of Christ (à Kempis), 30, 124
Inge, Ralph, 62, 83, 90, 110, 121
Introduction to the Devout Life (de Sales), 30, 42, 51
Irenaeus, 77, 86, 141n36

James, William, 83, 118
Jerome, 34
Jewish Kabbala, 101
Johnson, Samuel, 22, 117, 121, 122
Jones, R. M., 79, 82, 118
Journal (Wesley), 123, 124, 126, 127

Kaye, F. B., 60
Keble, John, 118
Kemp, Marjery, 132
à Kempis; *see* Thomas à Kempis
King's Cliffe, 13, 15, 16, 35, 81
Kingsley, Charles, 83
Kirk, Kenneth, 40, 139n43
Knox, Ronald, 20
Krapp, George, 109

La Bruyere, 110
Langcake, Thomas, 81
Latitudinarians, 21, 22, 58, 65, 130
Law, William, enduring achievement, 109; influence and general acclaim, 117–21; later works of devotion, 90; place in the literature of devotion 128–33

PROSE WORKS:

An Appeal to All Who Doubt the Truths of the Gospel, 71–72, 74
The Case of Reason or Natural Religion Fairly and Fully Stated, 64–65
Christian Perfection, 27, 33, 40, 112, 124, 133
A Collection of Letters on the Most Interesting and Important Subjects, 80

An Earnest and Serious Answer to Dr. Trapp's Discourse of the Folly, Sin, and Danger of Being Righteous Overmuch, 66–67
The Grounds and Reasons for Christian Regeneration, 69–71, 74
An Humble, Earnest, and Affectionate Address to the Clergy, 80–81
Letter to the Bishop of Bangor (first), 56
Letter to the Bishop of Bangor (second), 57
Letter to the Bishop of Bangor (third), 57–58
Of Justification by Faith and Works: a Dialogue between a Methodist and a Churchman, 72
Remarks upon a Late Book Entitled "The Fable of the Bees," 60–64
A Serious Call to a Devout and Holy Life, 27, 33, 40, 44, 50–51, 52, 120
A Short but Sufficient Confutation of the Reverend Dr. Warburton's Projected Defence of Christianity, 67–68
The Spirit of Love, 91–92, 101, 106, 108
The Spirit of Prayer, 87, 91, 92, 98–99, 101, 102, 105–107, 116
Three Letters to a Lady Inclined to Enter the Communion of the Church of Rome, 79–81
Unlawfulness of Stage Entertainment, 138n38
The Way to Divine Knowledge, 91, 93, 94, 97, 98, 101, 106–107
Letters and addresses, 79–81
Lettres Provinciales (Pascal), 59
Lewis, C. S., 72, 120
Locke, John, 21, 55
Luther, Martin, 77

McHugh, Helen, 34, 54, 109
MacNeill, John, 119
Malebranche, Nicholas, 13, 48, 69, 139n65
Mandeville, Bernard, 16, 60
Martin, Hugh, 119
Meditations (Hall), 51
Millar, John, 117
Milton, John, 104

Minor controversies: Trapp and Warburton, 66–68
Miranda, 36–37, 146n26
More, Henry, 62
Mysticism and Jacob Boehme, 82–90
Mysticism (definition), 82–86, 142n11

Nelson, Robert, 19
Nettleship, R. L., 83
Nondevotional works: controversy and theology, 55
Nonjuror, 14, 135n4, 17, 18, 22, 50, 56, 59, 127, 130

Okeley, Francis, 86, 119
Origen, 86
Overbury, Thomas, 114
Overton, John, 21, 46, 64, 90

Paley, William, 18
Pascal, Blaise, 110
Paternus, 37
Pathway unto Prayer (Becon), 42–4᳚
Pattison, Mark, 21, 63
Perry, G. G., 120
Physical appearance, 16–17
Pilgrim's Progress (Bunyan), 20
Plato, 13
Plotinus, 85
Pomander of Prayer (Becon), 43
Pope, Alexander, 22, 116
Prayer Book, 17, 46, 55
Private Devotions (Andrewes), 35
Psalm-singing, 45–46
Psalter, the, 42
Putney, 13, 123

Reasonableness of Christianity, The (Locke), 65
Reductio ad Absurdum, 111
Relton, Frederic, 22
Representation of the Committee (Hoadley), 57
Rolle, Richard, 48, 109
Rule for Anchoresses (Ancren Riwle), 34–35, 41

Saints' Everlasting Rest (Baxter), 20
Seven Forms of Nature, The, 70
Sizar, 13, 135n4

Smith, Henry, 109
Smith, John, 62
Society for the Publication of Christian Knowledge (SPCK), 19, 20
Special Times for Prayer, 46
Sperry, Willard, 128
Spiritual Combat (Scupoli), 42
Spurgeon, Caroline, 82, 83, 110, 131
Stage, the (Law's views), 39
Steele, Richard, 114
Stephen, Leslie, 50, 56, 64, 115, 133
Stillingfleet, Edward, 21
Stoudt, John, 88
Summa Theologica (Aquinas), 51
Suso, Henry, 69, 86, 94, 101
Swift, Jonathan, 22, 116

Talon, Henri, 112, 114
Tauler, Johannes, 69, 86, 87, 94, 101, 128
Taylor, Jeremy, 19, 31, 41, 46, 50, 129
Tenison, Thomas, 21
Theologica Germanica, 35, 49, 54, 86, 94, 96, 101, 123
Theological alterations, 73–79
Theophrastus, 114, 145n24
Theresa, Saint, 128
Thirty-nine Articles, 17, 18, 56, 58
Thomas à Kempis, 30, 48, 102, 104, 125, 129
Three rungs of the ladder of perfection, 84
Tindal, Matthew, 16, 64–65
Toleration Act of 1689, 17
Traditional themes: implementing doctrine, 49–50; injunctions to prayer, 42–47, 98–100; rigorous stewardship, 50–54; Scriptures and Christ as models for perfection, 29–34, 94–96; self-renunciation, 34–42, 96–98; union with God, 47–49, 92–94
Trapp, Joseph, 66, 86
Treaty of Utrecht, The, 13
Trevelyan, George, 19
Trinity in man, 74

Universalism (alleged), 75–76

"Vain and impertinent books," 38–40
Van Ruysbroeck, Jan, 49, 69, 86, 87, 94, 96
Variations in Law's thought, 89
Vaughan, Richard, 32

Walton, Christopher, 16, 53, 78–79, 87, 90, 121
Warburton, Bishop, 67–68
Ward, George, 81
Waterland, David, 22
Wesley, Charles, 126
Wesley, John, 14, 38, 77, 117, 125–128, 147n68
White, Helen, 24, 41, 109
Whole Duty of Man, The, (Cosin), 19
Whyte, Alexander, 16, 43, 90, 121
Williams, Charles, 118
Wilson, Colin, 110, 120
Wordsworth, William, 83
Works of theology, 68–73
Wren, Christopher, 19
Wright, Louis B., 42